A Manual for Writers

A Manual for Writers
of Research Papers, Theses, and Dissertations

Kate L. Turabian

First British Edition
Prepared by John E. Spink
Senior Lecturer, College of Librarianship Wales

Heinemann: London

William Heinemann Ltd
10 Upper Grosvenor Street, London W1X 9PA

LONDON MELBOURNE TORONTO
JOHANNESBURG AUCKLAND

First British publication 1982

© 1937, 1955, 1967, 1973
by the University of Chicago

Revised British edition © William Heinemann Ltd 1982

SBN 434 79970 X

Printed in Great Britain by
The Pitman Press, Bath

Contents

vi

Preface to the First British Edition

Those who have used Kate Turabian's *Manual* in the preparation of their own work or in the guidance of students have been impressed by the comprehensive nature of the work, by the good sense of her decisions and by the clarity of her examples. In preparing this first British edition I have endeavoured to interfere with her work as little as possible. I have occasionally rearranged paragraphs to bring British material into greater prominence and I have made alterations of detail to comply with British styles of citation. Only the section on the treatment of legal documents has required substantial revision. I have retained most of the American examples, as to change them would seem pedantic, especially since the American contribution to most fields of research is significant.

When in doubt, I have turned for guidance to the current editions of F. Howard Collins's *Authors and Printers Dictionary* and *Hart's Rules for Compositors and Readers* both of which are published by, and describe the practice of, the Oxford University Press.

The *Manual* is primarily directed at those who are preparing academic work to meet the requirements of institutions of higher learning, or who are presenting papers for publication in scholarly periodicals. It is hoped, however, that it will also provide guidance for those who are undertaking work at the secondary and further levels of education. It would greatly assist those who supervise the work of students at under- and post-graduate levels if students had gained experience in such formal presentation of work while at school.

In academic work there is no substitute for originality, for sound research and careful reasoning. Kate Turabian has stressed in her Preface to the original work that "the ideas, the findings, and the conclusions put forth in the paper are of prime importance". Good presentation and meticulous bibliographical citation cannot make up for lack of these. The fact remains, however, that they do enhance a sound piece of academic work and that neglect of them brings the other aspects of a writer's work under suspicion.

Finally, I have to acknowledge the help that I have received from so many of my friends and colleagues at the College of Librarianship Wales. They gave their time and expertise willingly, and I am especially grateful to Denis Grogan, who read most of the text, and to Bernard Mineur, who revised the legal section. It is necessary to stress, however, that any flaws in the text are of my own making. The outstanding qualities of the *Manual* remain a testimony to the labour of love sustained over many years by Kate L. Turabian.

John E. Spink

1 The Parts of the Paper

1:1   A paper[1] is normally made up of three main parts: the preliminaries, the text, and the reference matter. In a long paper each of these main parts may consist of several sections (see below); but in a short paper there may be nothing more than a title page and text, the latter with or without subheadings, tables, illustrations, as the topic and treatment may require. The inclusion of a table or two, an illustration or two, does not automatically call for a list of tables and a list of illustrations; and for some papers a table of contents may have little value. These are matters, however, that must be left to the good sense of the writer, who should know best what arrangements are suitable for his particular piece of work.

1:2   The *order* of the following outline, regardless of the parts that may be omitted, should be observed. (Note that a table of contents and a list of illustrations or tables come before the preface.)

The preliminaries:

Frontispiece (see para. 11:4)

Title page

Blank page

Table of contents

List of illustrations

List of tables

---

[1]The term 'paper' is used throughout this *Manual* to refer alike to research papers, reports, theses, and dissertations, except in matters relating specifically to one of them.

Preface, including acknowledgements, or acknowledgements alone unless these appear as the final paragraph in the paper

The text:

Introduction

Main body of the paper, usually consisting of well-defined divisions, such as parts, chapters, sections, etc., and including footnotes

The reference matter:

Appendix or Appendices

Bibliography

Additional reference material, such as a glossary or a list of abbreviations devised specifically for use in the paper

THE PRELIMINARIES

TITLE PAGE

1:3 Some universities and colleges have their own style of title page for theses and dissertations, and this should be followed exactly in matters of content and spacing. For papers and reports, if a sample sheet is not provided, a title page might logically include the name of the university or college (usually centred at the top of the sheet), the exact title of the paper, the course, the date, and the name of the writer—all suitably capitalized, centred, and spaced upon the page. A sample title page will be found at the end of this chapter (Sample A.)

TABLE OF CONTENTS

1.4 The table of contents, sometimes headed simply "Contents", includes the list of illustrations, list of tables, preface (or acknowledgements), introduction, chapters (or their equivalents) with their numbers and titles, appendix (or appendices) and bibliography, with the page numbers of each. If the chapters are grouped under "parts", the numbers and titles (if any) of the parts also appear in the contents. Subheadings within the chapters are frequently included, in one of various ways, or they may be omitted entirely from the table of contents. Four styles of tables of contents are shown in samples B–E following this chapter. (Note that none of these samples gives the complete contents of a paper. For suggestions on spacing and other matters related to typing the table of contents, see paras. 13:14–16.)

1:5   In preparing a table of contents for a paper containing sub-headings of one or more levels (see para. 1:18), there is great latitude in choosing both the amount of information included and the method of presenting it. At one extreme, the contents may provide what is essentially an outline by including all the levels (sample C). At the other extreme, the contents may omit the subheadings (even though the paper may carry subheadings of one level or more than one) showing only the chapter numbers and titles. For many papers, both those with only one level and those with more than one level of subheadings, the contents includes the first-level (principal) subheadings, with or without the page numbers (sample B). Note that when more than one level of subheading is included in the contents, each must appear in order of its rank; that is, it is not permissible to begin with any but the first-level, or to skip from the first- to the third- or fourth-level.

1:6   As for the method of including subheadings in the contents, if more than one level is shown, each level is indented three spaces below the preceding higher level (sample C). If only the first-level is shown, each subheading may be indented three spaces below the chapter title (sample B), or, if the subheadings are short, the first one in each chapter is indented three spaces below the chapter title and the following ones are run in (samples D and E). Punctuation separating run-in subheadings may be semicolons, dashes, or periods. (For page numbers with subheadings, see para. 1:10.)

1:7   The wording of part and chapter titles and of all subheadings should follow exactly their wording within the body of the paper, although the capitalization of subheadings, as indicated below (para. 1:8), may differ from that appearing in the text.

1:8   *Capitalization* of titles in the table of contents should be as follows: for the titles of all major divisions (contents, list of

3

illustrations, list of tables, preface, introduction, parts, chapters, appendix, bibliography), capitalize all letters (e.g., PREFACE). Subheadings may be capitalized in one of two ways: (1) capitalize the initial letter of the first and last words and of all words except articles, prepositions, and coordinate conjunctions (sample E); or (2) capitalize only the initial letter of the first subheading under the chapter and of proper nouns and proper adjectives (sample D).

1:9   *Numbers* designating parts and chapters should be given as they are in the text. Part numbers may be capital roman numerals (PART I, PART II, etc.) or spelled-out numbers (PART ONE, PART TWO, etc.). The number may precede the part title and be separated from it by a full stop (sample B) or it may be centred above the title and thus need no punctuation (sample D). Chapter numbers may be arabic or capital roman numerals or spelled-out numbers. The word "Chapter" is sometimes included with the number (sample E) or is placed over all the chapter numbers (samples B and C) or it may be omitted (sample D). Do not use the word "Chapter" in the contents if the sections of the paper are not so designated.

1:10   *Page numbers* in a typed table of contents are always given at the right-hand side of the page, each following a line of dots (leaders) from the title of the section. Note that only the *beginning* page number of each chapter or other section is given. Page numbers for parts may be omitted unless they are not evidenced by the beginning page number of the first chapter under each part. Note that if the page number is given for one part, it must be given for all of them. Page numbers for subheadings may also be omitted; when they are included with run-in subheadings, they are best placed within parentheses immediately following the subheadings (sample E). (For alignment of leaders and page numbers, see para. 13:14.)

LIST OF ILLUSTRATIONS

1:11   A list of illustrations, sometimes headed simply "Illustrations", consists of the figure numbers (indicated with arabic numerals), the legends (titles) of all the figures, and the page numbers. The legends should agree with those given under the illustrations, although if they are long it is usually permissible to give them in shortened form in the list. If a descriptive or explanatory statement appears in addition to the legend under the illustration, there should be no hesitancy about omitting such a statement in the list of illustrations. (See sample F).

1:12   In the list of illustrations, *but not under the illustrations* (para. 11:8), the legends are typed in capital and small letters (i.e., capitalize the initial letter of the first and last words and all words except articles, prepositions, and coordinate conjunctions). If, in addition to illustrations called figures, there are others designated specifically as maps or charts or graphs (e.g., Map 1), these should be included in the list of illustrations, in separate sections under their designated labels (see sample G).

LIST OF TABLES

1:13   A list of tables gives the table numbers with their respective titles and page numbers. The titles as shown in the list should agree exactly with their wording above the tables themselves. Table numbers are expressed in arabic numerals, and the titles are typed in capital and small letters, as for legends in the list of illustrations (see para. 1:12 and sample H).

PREFACE (OR ACKNOWLEDGEMENTS)

1:14   Included in the preface are such matters as the writer's reasons for making the study, its background, scope, and purpose, and an acknowledgement of the aids afforded him in the process of the research and writing by institutions and persons. If the writer thinks he has nothing significant to say about the study that is not covered in the main body of the paper and wishes only to acknowledge the various sorts of assistance that he has received, he should entitle his remarks "Acknowledgements" rather than "Preface".

THE TEXT

INTRODUCTION

1:15   The text ordinarily begins with an introduction, which may be chapter 1. If it is short, the writer may prefer to head it simply "Introduction" and reserve the more formal heading "Chapter" for the longer sections of which the main body of the paper is composed. But the introduction, whether it is called chapter 1 or not, is the first major division of the text, not the last of the preliminaries, as is sometimes supposed. Thus the first page of the introduction is page 1 (arabic numeral) of the paper.

CHAPTERS OR THEIR EQUIVALENTS

1:16   The main body of the paper is usually divided into chapters, each chapter having a title and each beginning on a new page. In a short paper some writers prefer to omit the word "Chapter" and to use merely numerals, roman or arabic, in sequence before the headings of the several main divisions. In a long paper some writers like to group related chapters into "parts", with or without individual titles (see sample B). In that case, each part is preceded by a part-title page.

PART-TITLE PAGES

1:17   Part-title pages (sometimes referred to as half-title pages) are required if the chapters are grouped under "parts", the part-title page being placed immediately before the first chapter of the group composing the part. Since the introduction is to the *entire* paper, whether or not it is titled "Chapter 1", it is not included in "Part I". The first part-title page therefore follows rather than precedes the introduction.

SUBHEADINGS

1:18   In some papers the chapters or their equivalents are divided into sections, which may in turn be divided into subsections, and these into sub-subsections, and so on. Such divisions are customarily given titles, called *subheadings,* which are designated respectively *first-, second-,* and *third-level* subheadings and differentiated from one another by typing style. The style of subheading with the greatest attention value should be given to the principal, or first-level, subdivision. On a typewritten page centred headings have greater attention value than side headings, and underlined headings, centred or side, have greater attention value than those not underlined. A plan for the display of five levels of subheadings in a typed paper follows:

First-level, centred heading, underlined:

<u>Traditional Controversy between Medieval
Church and State</u>

Second-level, centred heading, not underlined:

Reappearance of Religious Legalism

Third-level, side heading underlined, beginning at the left margin:

<u>Jesus and Paul</u>

Fourth-level, side heading, not underlined:

The Gospel as initiated
by Jesus

Fifth-level, heading run into (at the beginning of) a paragraph and underlined:

<u>The gospel legalized in the Church</u>. The gospel that was offered by the early Christians to the pagans . . . was made available through the Church.

Note that first- and second-level subheadings are typed in capital and small letters (i.e., first and last words and all other words except articles, prepositions, and coordinate conjunctions capitalized), and that lower-level subheadings capitalize only the first word, proper nouns, and proper adjectives.

1:19   If fewer than five levels are required, they may be selected in any suitable *descending order,* as indicated above. (For spacing subheadings see paras. 13:24–25.)

FOOTNOTES

1:20   Footnotes, also considered part of the text, are discussed in chapter 6.

THE REFERENCE MATTER

APPENDIX

1:21   An appendix, although by no means an essential part of every paper, is a useful device to make available to the reader material related to the text but not suitable for inclusion in it. Such material may be: tables too detailed for text presentation; technical notes on method, and schedules and forms used in collecting materials; copies of documents not generally available to the reader; case studies too long to be put into the text; and sometimes figures or other illustrative materials.

1:22   If the materials relegated to an appendix are numerous and fall into several categories, each category should form a separate appendix. Where there is more than one appendix, each should be given a number or a letter (Appendix 1, Appendix 2, etc.; or, Appendix A, Appendix B, etc.).

1:23   The writer may use his discretion about whether a single appendix should carry a title, like a chapter title. If there is more than one appendix, however, each should carry a descriptive title.

1:24   Whether to type an appendix in single or double space depends upon the nature of the material; spacing need not be the same for all the appendices. Documents and case studies may well be in single space, whereas explanations of methods and procedures may be in double space, like the text, for instance.

GLOSSARY

1:25   If a paper contains many foreign words or technical words and phrases not likely to be familiar to the reader, a list of these words, with their translations or definitions, will be helpful. The words should be arranged in alphabetical order, as in a dictionary. Each word should be typed flush with the left margin and followed by a comma or a colon and the translation or definition. Any runover lines should be indented three spaces. If any of the definitions consists of one or more sentences, all entries should end with a full stop. If all definitions consist only of words or phrases, no final punctuation should be used. Double space should appear between items.

LIST OF ABBREVIATIONS

1:26 A list of abbreviations at the end of a paper is desirable only if the author has used a number of arbitrarily devised abbreviations in his footnotes or elsewhere. It is not necessary to list commonly accepted abbreviations, such as those used for the titles of journals in various fields. Any such list should, like a glossary, be arranged in alphabetical order, that is by the abbreviation itself, not its spelled-out form. The punctuation and typing style of the list should be the same as that recommended for a glossary (para. 1:25).

BIBLIOGRAPHY

1:27 The bibliography is the last section of the paper (except in those rare instances, such as a book, where a paper carries an index). Instructions for the preparation and style of a bibliography are set forth in chapters 7 and 8.

SAMPLE A. Title page for a dissertation.

THE UNIVERSITY OF CHICAGO

INTERNAL RELATEDNESS AND PLURALISM IN THE
PHILOSOPHY OF WHITEHEAD

A DISSERTATION SUBMITTED TO
THE FACULTY OF THE DIVISION OF THE HUMANITIES
IN CANDIDACY FOR THE DEGREE OF
DOCTOR OF PHILOSOPHY

DEPARTMENT OF PHILOSOPHY

BY
WILLIAM PAINE ALSTON

CHICAGO, ILLINOIS
MARCH 1951

SAMPLE B. Partial table of contents for a work in which chapters are grouped under "parts". First-level subheadings only are shown and their individual page numbers are omitted. (See para. 1:5.)

TABLE OF CONTENTS

SAMPLE C. Partial table of contents showing three levels of subheadings with page numbers. Note that turnover lines in subheadings are indented to the third space.

TABLE OF CONTENTS

12

SAMPLE D. Partial table of contents in which only first-level subheadings are shown, run in under chapter headings, and individual page numbers omitted.

CONTENTS

SAMPLE E. Partial table of contents in which first-level subheadings, each with its beginning page number, are run in under chapter headings.

CONTENTS

SAMPLE F. List of illustrations, all of which are the same type.

SAMPLE G. List of illustrations in which two types are shown.

SAMPLE H. List of tables, showing the number of the table, the title, and the page number.

LIST OF TABLES

2 Abbreviations, Contractions and Numbers

ABBREVIATIONS AND CONTRACTIONS

2:1   The distinction between them is that abbreviations may consist of one or more letters of the full word but always lack its final letter, whereas contractions always retain the final letter. Abbreviations should end with a full stop:

M. MM. Co. Rev. st. (stanza) fig. f. ff. p. pp.

Contractions should have no full stop:

Mr Mrs Dr St (Saint or Street) Ltd Mme Messrs ft 1st

Abbreviations and contractions *in text,* except in scientific and technical writing, have long been frowned upon. In footnotes and bibliographies, in tabular matter, and in some kinds of illustrations (e.g., maps, graphs, charts), however, they not only are permitted but are normally preferred. Also, there are a few words that are almost never spelled out.

WITH PERSONAL NAMES

2:2   Use the following for social titles before names: Mr, Messrs, Mrs, Mlle, M., MM., Mme, Sr, and corresponding abbreviations in other foreign languages.

2:3   Use the contraction Dr before a name, but spell out the word *doctor* when it appears without a name:

Dr Bixby came at once.

The doctor was out of town.

2:4   Use abbreviations for scholastic degrees and professional affiliations after names: M.A., Ph.D., Litt.D., M.D.,

16

F.R.S., and so on. A comma precedes such an abbreviation when it follows a name:

Thomas Q. Donne, Ph.D.

2:5   Use the forms Sr, Jr, II, III (for Senior, Junior, Second, Third), following a full name. Never use the spelled-out words or the abbreviations with the surname alone. (In informal writing it is permissible to use the terms with given names.) Note that a comma precedes Jr and Sr, but not II, III:

Christopher Morley, Jr   Mrs Joseph P. Turner, Sr

but: Abraham Darby I

2:6   Spell out a civil, military, professional, or religious title when it precedes the surname alone:

Professor Gale   General Fairweather   Father Kennedy

But use the appropriate abbreviation before a full name:

Brig. Gen. Thomas Fairweather   Prof. Gordon Gale

2:7   Spell out *Reverend* and *Honourable* if preceded by *the*; otherwise abbreviate to Rev. and Hon. Never use the title, either spelled out or abbreviated, with the surname alone, but only when it is followed by the person's full name, or by Mr or Dr as may be appropriate:

Wrong: Rev. Bentley (or the Rev. Bentley)

Right: Rev. John Bentley (or the Reverend John
         Bentley, or the Reverend Dr Bentley, or
         Rev. Dr Bentley)

2:8   *Saint* standing before the name of a saint may be abbreviated, St (plural, SS.):

St Thomas Aquinas   SS. Augustine and Benedict

2:9   Names preceded by *Saint* are spelled out or abbreviated, as personal preference on the part of the bearers of such names may determine:

Etienne Geoffroy Saint-Hilaire

Louis Stephen St Laurent

BOOKS OF THE BIBLE

2:10   Spell out the names of the books of the Bible and of the Apocrypha, except when they occur with exact references.

2:11   Acceptable abbreviations may be found in the preliminary matter of the Bible and in the *Shorter Oxford English Dictionary.* Place a colon between chapter and verse number(s).

Some Bible scholars do not believe that the Gospel of John was written by the Apostle John.

The Beatitudes are found in Matt. 5:3-12.

GEOGRAPHIC NAMES

2:12   Spell out the names of countries (except that USSR is now commonly used for Union of Socialist Soviet Republics), counties, provinces, territories, bodies of water, mountains, and the like.

2:13   Spell out the prefixes of geographic names: Fort, Lake, Mount, Point, Port, Saint:

Mount Prospect   Saint Louis

2:14   Spell out all such words as *avenue, street, drive, road, court, square, terrace, building,* capitalizing only when they are used as part of a name:

Many members of staff live in Bryant Terrace.

Charming Georgian houses stand in the old square.

2:15   Spell out *north, south, east, west,* as well as *north-east, south-west,* and so on, capitalizing when they are part of a name, and abbreviating when they follow a street name:

The seminary is in West Newton, Massachusetts.

The shop is at 245 Seventeenth Street NW.

High-rise flats are going up on the north-west side of the city.

TIME

2:16   Spell out the names of months and of days when they occur in text, whether alone or in dates. But in footnotes, bibliographies, tables (and other closely set matter), the following designations are permissible if used consistently: Jan., Feb., Mar., Apr., May, June, July, Aug., Sept., Oct., Nov., Dec.; Sun., Mon., Tues., Wed., Thurs., Fri., Sat.

2:17   Use the abbreviations a.m., p.m., after numerals indicating time of day. (see para. 2:42).

2:18   For era designations use the abbreviations B.C. and A.D. ("before Christ", "anno Domini"). A.D. should precede the year number, and B.C. should follow it:

> Solomon's Temple was destroyed by the Babylonians in 587 B.C. Rebuilt in 515 B.C., it was destroyed by the Romans in A.D. 70.

MEASUREMENTS

2:19   Spell out expressions of dimension, distance, measure, weight, degree, and so on (but see para. 2:50).

PARTS OF A BOOK

2:20   Spell out the words *book, chapter, part, volume, section, scene, verse, column, page, figure, plate,* and so on, except that, when such a term is followed by a number in footnote and parenthetical material, abbreviation is preferred: bk(s), chap(s)., pt(s), vol(s)., sec(s)., sc., v. (vv.), col(s)., p. (pp.), fig(s)., pl(s). The words *act, line,* and *table* should never be abbreviated.

ORGANIZATIONS

2:21   It is now general practice to refer to many government agencies, unions, public bodies, and so on, by the initials of their names, omitting full stops. For unfamiliar abbreviations, the name should be spelled out at its first occurrence and the abbreviation placed in parentheses immediately after. Following are some of the better-known abbreviations:

BBC	BMA	YMCA
NATO	RIBA	CIA
TUC	UN	UGC

Note the exceptions: Aslib (not ASLIB), Unesco (not UNESCO).

2:22   Some abbreviations should be used in giving the names of companies, even though the individual firm name does not abbreviate the word: &, Bro., Bros, Co., Corp. *The* before a name, and *Inc.* or *Ltd* following it, are usually omitted; when *the* is needed in the context, it is not treated as part of the title and therefore is not capitalized:

```
The book was published by the University of
Chicago Press.
```

NUMBERS

GENERAL RULE

2:23   In scientific material all measurements are expressed in figures (para. 2:49). In non-scientific material, numbers are sometimes spelled out and sometimes expressed in figures, according to prescribed rules. The general rule followed by many writers is to spell out all numbers up through one hundred—e.g., sixty-five, ninety-eight—and all round numbers that can be expressed in two words—e.g., one hundred, two hundred, five thousand, forty-five hundred:

```
At that time the population of Israel was less than
three million.
```

Exact numbers over one hundred are written as figures:

```
There were 614 secondary school children involved
in the experiment.
```

SERIES

2:24   The general rule requires modification when numbers above *and* below one hundred appear in a series, or group, of numbers each of which applies to the same kind of thing. Here all are expressed in figures:

```
In the area studied, there were 186 such buildings,
the smaller housing anything from 50 to 65 persons
each, and the larger from 650 to 900 each, with a
single room sometimes occupied by 8 to 10.
```

INITIAL NUMBERS

2:25   A sentence should never begin with a figure, even when there are figures in the rest of the sentence. Either spell out the first number or, better, recast the sentence:

Two hundred and fifty passengers escaped injury;
175 sustained minor injuries; 110 were so seriously
hurt that they required hospitalization.
<u>Or, better</u>:
There were 250 passengers who escaped injury;
175 who sustained minor injuries; and 110 who were
so seriously hurt that they required hospitalization.

ROUND NUMBERS

2:26   Although round numbers occurring in isolation are spelled
out (para. 2:23), several round numbers occurring close
together are usually expressed in figures:

There were 1,500 books in the first shipment, 8,000
in the second, and 100,000 in the third; altogether
there were now about 1,000,000 volumes in the ware-
house.

2:27   Very large round numbers are frequently expressed in figures
and units of millions or billions:

This means that Japan will require about 7.8 million
barrels of oil a day compared with 3.2 million
barrels a day in current consumption.

PERCENTAGES AND DECIMALS

2:28   Figures should be used to express decimals and percentages.
The words *per cent* should be written out, except in scientific
writing, where the symbol % may be used:

With interest at 8 per cent, the monthly payment
would amount to £12.88, which, he noted, was exactly
2.425 times the amount he was accustomed to save
monthly.

FRACTIONS

2:29   A fraction standing alone should be spelled out, but a
numerical unit composed of a whole number and a fraction
should be expressed in figures:

Trade and commodity services accounted for nine-
tenths of all international receipts and payments.

Cabinets with $10\frac{1}{2}$-by-$32\frac{1}{4}$-inch shelves were installed.

21

MONEY

2:30   *British currency.* Since decimalization came into effect in February 1971, British currency has been expressed in pounds and pence:

two pounds   twenty-five pence

£3.50   25p.

Before decimalization, British currency was expressed in pounds, shillings, and pence:

threepence   seventeen shillings   four pounds

two shillings and sixpence

£12.17s. 6d.   <u>or</u>   £12.17.6   £48 million

£1,238 million

A sum of money might also be expressed in *guineas* (twenty-one shillings equalled a guinea):

thirty guineas (gns)   342 guineas

2:31   *United States currency.* The general rule (para. 2:23) applies in isolated references to amounts of money in United States currency. If the amount is spelled out, so are the words *dollars* and *cents*; if figures are used, the dollar symbol ($) precedes them:

Rarely do they spend more than five dollars a week on recreation.

But:
The report showed $135 collected in fines.

Fractional amounts of money over one dollar appear in figures like other decimal fractions ($1.75). When both fractional amounts and whole-dollar amounts are used in the same sentence (and only in such circumstances), the whole-dollar amounts are shown with a decimal point and ciphers:

The same article is sold by some stores for $1.75, by others for $1.95, and by still others for $2.00.

2:32   The expression of very large amounts of money, which may be cumbersome whether spelled out in full or written in figures, may well follow the rule for expressing large round numbers (para. 2:27), using units of millions or billions with figures preceded by the dollar sign:

> Japan's exports to Taiwan, which averaged $60 million
> between 1954 and 1958, rose sharply to $210 million
> in 1965, and $250 million in 1966.

> The deficit that year was $10.4 billion.

2:33   *Other foreign currencies.* Most foreign currencies follow a system like that of Britain, employing unit symbols before the figures. They do vary, however, in their expressions of large numbers and decimals.

PARTS OF WRITTEN WORKS

2:34   With few exceptions, all the numbered parts of printed works are cited in arabic numerals. If, however, a reference is made to the preliminary pages of a work that designates those pages with small roman numerals, the reference should also employ that style.

2:35   Citations to official publications and manuscript material should use exactly the kind of numerals found in the source.

DATES

2:36   *Day, month, and year.* One of the two permissible styles for expressing day, month, and year should be followed consistently throughout the paper. The first, in which punctuation is omitted, is preferred:

> On 28 June 1970 the Convocation <u>Pacem in Maribus</u>
> was convened.

> Or:
> On June 28, 1970, the Convocation <u>Pacem in Maribus</u>
> was convened.

2:37   When the day, month, and year are mentioned as in the foregoing examples, note that *st, d,* or *th* does not appear after the day. But when the day alone is given, or when the day is separated from the month by one or more words, the preferred style is to spell out the day of the month:

> The date set was the twenty-ninth.

> The sequence of events of the tenth of June is
> unclear.

> Or:
> The sequence of events of 10 June is unclear.

2:38   When month and year alone are mentioned, the preferred style is to omit punctuation between them: June 1970.

2:39   In informal writing it is permissible to abbreviate reference to the year:

> It would certainly appear that the May '79
> election did not strengthen the Liberal position.

2:40   *Centuries.* References to particular centuries should be spelled out, uncapitalized:

> the eighteenth century   the mid-twentieth century
>
> seventeenth-century literature

2:41   *Decades.* References to decades take two forms. The context sometimes determines the one chosen:

> The 1890s saw an enormous increase in the use of
> manufactured gas.
>
> During the thirties traffic decreased by 50 per cent.

TIME OF DAY

2:42   Except when a.m. or p.m. is used, time of day should be spelled out in text matter. Never add *in the morning* after a.m. or *in the evening* after p.m., and never use *o'clock* with either a.m. or p.m. or with figures. Write, for example:

> The train was due to arrive at 7.10 a.m.
>
> The meeting was called for 8.00 p.m.
>
> Or:
> The meeting was called for eight o'clock in the
> evening.

Where the context makes clear whether it is morning or evening that is meant, you might write simply:

> The meeting was called for eight o'clock.
>
> The night operator takes calls from eleven to seven.

NUMBERS WITH NAMES

2:43   *Rulers.* In a succession of emperors, kings, queens, or popes with the same name, identification is by numerals, traditionally capital roman:

24

```
Charles V        Henry VIII      Elizabeth II
Napoleon III     Louis XIV       John XXIII
```

2:44   *Family names.* Male members of families with identical names are sometimes differentiated in the same way as monarchs:

```
Adlai E. Stevenson III
```

See also paragraph 2:5.

2:45   *Governmental   designations.*   Particular   dynasties, governments, governing bodies, and political divisions are commonly designated by an ordinal number before the noun and are capitalized. Numerals of less than one hundred should be spelled out; those over one hundred, written in figures:

```
Nineteenth Dynasty
Fifth Republic
Third Reich
```

2:46   *Churches, lodges, unions.* Numerals standing before the names of churches or religious organizations are usually spelled-out ordinals:

```
Eighteenth Church of Christ, Scientist
Seventh Day Adventists
```

2:47   *Military regiments and formations.* Numbers of regiments, divisions, squadrons and other military formations should be expressed in arabic numerals:

```
1st Royal Tank Regiment
6th SS Panzer Army
92nd Fighter Squadron, Royal Air Force
17th Airborne Division, United States Army
```

2:48   *Street addresses, motorways* and *roads, telephone numbers.* It is preferable to spell out the names of numbered streets under one hundred for the sake of appearance and ease of reading, but street (as well as building) addresses, motorway and highway numbers, and telephone numbers should be expressed in figures.

SCIENTIFIC USAGE

2:49   In mathematical, statistical, technical, or scientific text, where physical quantities for distances, lengths, areas, volumes, pressures, and so on, are frequently referred to, all amounts should be expressed in figures, whether they are under or over one hundred:

```
30 millilitres      2,200 miles
3 cubic feet        125 volts
12 metres           10 picas
60 pounds           10°C, 10.5°C
180 hectares        10° (of arc)
```

2:50 Note also in technical writing that abbreviations (usually without full stops) may be used for distance, length, area, volume, weight, and so on, if the amount is given in numerals:

```
113 g    50 lb       8.3 ft
32 oz    25 ml       15 kW
137 mm   25-30 min   15 cm²
```

THE COMMA WITH NUMBERS

2:51 For the most part, in numbers of one thousand or more, the thousands are marked off with commas:

```
1,500      12,275,500      1,475,525,000
```

No comma is used, however, in page numbers, telephone numbers, four-digit year numbers and the like, and decimal fractions of less than one.

Note, however, that in year dates of more than four figures, the comma is employed: 10,000 B.C.

CONTINUED NUMBERS

2:52 The term *continued numbers* (or *inclusive numbers*) refers to the first and last number of a sequence of numerical designations, such as pages or years. Continued numbers are separated by a hyphen in a typewritten work and expressed according to the following scheme, which is based on the way one normally speaks these numbers:

First Number	Second Number	Examples
Less than 100	Use all digits	3-10; 71-72

100 or multiple	Use all digits	100–104; 600–613
More than 100 but less than 110 (in multiples of 100)	Use changed part only (i.e., omit 0)	107–8; 1002–3
More than 109 (in multiples of 100)	Use last two digits (or all if more than last two digits change)	321–25; 415–532; 1536–38; 1890–1954

The principal use of the foregoing scheme is for page numbers and other numbered parts of written works, and for inclusive year dates:

pp. 2–14, 45–46, 125–26, 200–210, 308–9

the years 1933–36 of the Great Depression

the Napoleonic victories of 1800–1801

PLURALS

2:53   Plurals of numbers expressed in figures are formed by the addition of *s* alone (i.e., not apostrophe and *s*):

DC 10s continued to be flown.

AACR2s were issued to all students.

IBM 360s were used throughout the company.

2:54   Plurals of spelled-out numbers are formed like the plurals of other nouns:

There were many more twelves and fourteens than thirty-twos, thirty-fours, and thirty-sixes on sale.

Most of the women were in their thirties or forties.

ENUMERATIONS

2:55   *Run on in text.* Numbers (or letters) used to enumerate items in text stand out better when they are set in parentheses, either double or single, than when they are followed by periods:

He gave three reasons for his resignation: (1) age, 63, (2) gradually failing eyesight, and (3) desire to live under less pressure.

2:56 *Beginning a new line or paragraph.* When numbered items in an enumeration without subdivisions begin each on a new line, they are most often indicated by arabic numerals followed by a full stop. The items may be treated like the paragraphs of the text, that is, given paragraph indention with the turnover lines begun at the margin:

```
    1. The nature of the relationship between
library quality and library use
```

Or they may be set flush with the margin, and the turnover lines aligned with the first line of substantive matter:

```
    9.  Selective initial dissemination of published
        material--a direct responsibility of the library

   10.  Arrangement and organization of the collection
```

In both styles, full stops following numerals must be aligned. Full stops at the ends of lines should be omitted, whether or not the items are composed of complete sentences (see para. 3:55).

2:57 *In outline form.* For an outline or other enumeration in which there are subdivisions, the following scheme of notation and indention is recommended. It is not necessary to use a capital roman numeral for the first level when there are fewer divisions than shown in the example. The first level may well begin with A or with 1 (arabic one):

```
     I.  Wars of the Nineteenth Century
         A.  United States
             1.  Civil War, 1861-65
                 a)  Causes
                     (1)  Slavery
                         (a)  Compromise
                             i)  Missouri Compromise
                             ii)  Compromise of 1850

    II.  Under the head of . . .
         A.  Under the head of . . .
             1.  Under the head of . . .
```

28

3 Spelling and Punctuation

SPELLING

3:1   Spelling should accord with the best British usage and must be consistent, except in quotations, where the original must be followed exactly. The authority recommended for spelling and for syllabication (which generally determines the division of words at the end of lines) is the current edition of F. Howard Collins's *Authors and Printers Dictionary*. For the spelling of personal names, reference should be made to *Chambers's Biographical Dictionary,* and of geographical names, to Chambers's *World Gazetteer and Geographical Dictionary.*

PLURALS

3:2   *Proper names*. Plurals of the names of persons and of other capitalized names are formed by the addition of *s* or *es* without the change of a final *y* to *i* as required for common nouns.

3:3   Add *s* to all names except those ending in *s, x,* or *z,* or in *ch* or *sh*:

the Andersons	the Costellos	the Frys
the Bradleys	the Joyces	the Pettees

3:4   Add *es* to names ending in *s, x,* or *z,* or in *ch* or *sh*:

the Rosses	the Coxes	the Marshes
the Jenkinses	the Rodriguezes	the Finches

3:5   *Capital letters*. Form the plurals of most single and multiple capital letters used as nouns by adding *s* alone:

```
The three Rs are taught at the two YMCAs.
```

3:6   *Small letters.* Form the plurals of all small letters, of capital letters with full stops, and of capital letters that would be confusing if *s* alone were added, by adding an apostrophe and *s*:

```
All the examples were labelled by letter; the a's
were tested first, the b's second, and so on.

The B.A.'s and B.Sc.'s conferred were almost ten
times the number of M.A.'s, M.Sc.'s, and Ph.D.'s.

The A's, I's, and S's in the directory were checked
by one group.
```

POSSESSIVES

3:7   Form the possessive case of a proper name in the singular by adding an apostrophe and *s*:

```
Jones's book       Marx's ideology
Stevens's poems    Diaz's revolt
Kinross's farm     Finch's candidacy
```

But see the exceptions noted below (3:8 and 9):

3:8   The possessive case of the names of Jesus and Moses, and of Greek (or hellenized) names of more than one syllable ending in *es*, is formed by adding an apostrophe alone:

```
Jesus' ministry     Aristophanes' plays
Moses' leadership   Xerxes' victories
```

3:9   For some common nouns as well, a regard for euphony sets aside the rule for forming the possessive by adding an apostrophe and *s*, and instead adds only an apostrophe:

```
for conscience' sake      for appearance' sake
for righteousness' sake
```

3:10   Form the possessive case of a plural proper name (the Bradleys, the Costellos, etc.) by adding an apostrophe to the accepted form of the plural of the name. (See paras. 3.3 and 4.)

```
the Bradleys' house     the Rodriguezes' mine
the Costellos' ranch    the Finches' yacht
```

30

PLURALS AND POSSESSIVES OF PREPOSITIONAL-PHRASE COMPOUNDS

3:11   Note that although the plurals of prepositional-phrase compounds are formed according to the rule governing the first noun of the compound, as, for example:

```
brothers-in-law    commanders-in-chief    men-of-war
```

the possessive case of the same compound words is:

```
my brother-in-law's business
the commander-in-chief's dispatches
the man-of-war's launching
```

COMPOUND WORDS

3:12   The hyphen is used in many compound words; but which should be hyphenated, which left open, and which spelled as one word is a thorny question. F. Howard Collins's *Authors and Printers Dictionary* gives the answer for most noun forms and for many adjective forms. Nevertheless, there are still some noun forms and a good many adjective forms that are not included in the dictionary. Principles of hyphenation for some of these are given in the following paragraphs:

3:13   Compounds made up of a word of relationship plus a noun should be spelled as separate words:

```
brother officer       mother church
father figure         parent organization
foster child          sister ship
```

3:14   Compounds made up of two nouns that are different but of equal importance should be hyphenated:

```
author-critic         artist-inventor
composer-director     architect-painter
city-state            scholar-poet
```

3:15   Compounds ending with *-elect* should be hyphenated except when the name of the office is in two or more words:

```
president-elect    but:    county clerk elect
```

3:16   Combinations of words including a prepositional phrase that describe a character should be hyphenated:

```
stay-at-home          stick-in-the-mud
Alice-sit-by-the-fire Puss-in-boots
```

31

3:17   When spelled out, fractional numbers should be hyphenated unless either numerator or denominator already contains a hyphen:

```
two-thirds        but:   six and two-thirds
one-half                 sixty-five hundredths
```

3:18   Many compounds ending with *-book* have been accepted into the general English vocabulary as single words; others are treated as two words:

```
textbook          but:   telephone book
wordbook                 pattern book
workbook                 Note the exceptions:
                         cheque-book, in English
                         usage, (checkbook in
                         American usage), and
                         guide-book.
```

3:19   The same applies to compounds ending in *-house*:

```
clubhouse         but:   business house
greenhouse               rest house
```

3:20   Spell as separate words adjective forms composed of an adverb ending in *-ly* plus an adjective or a participle:

```
highly developed species    barely breathing bird
newly minted coins          easily seen result
```

3:21   Adjective forms composed of unhyphenated proper names should be written as separate words:

```
Old French            Modern Greek
Latin American        New Testament
```

3:22   Compounds with *better-, best-, ill-, lesser-, little-, well-,* and the like, should be hyphenated when they precede the noun unless there is a modifier:

```
better-paid job         little-expected aid
best-liked teacher      well-intentioned man
ill-advised step   but: a very well intentioned man
lesser-known evil
```

As predicate adjectives they are generally spelled as two words:

```
The step was ill advised. It was clear that the man
was well intentioned.
```

3:23   An adjective form composed of a present participle preceded by its object should be hyphenated:

```
emotion-producing            thought-provoking
dissension-arousing          vote-getting
```

Noun forms similarly constructed are generally treated as two words:

```
decision making              problem solving
coal mining                  food gathering
```

3:24 Chemical terms used as adjectives are spelled as two words, unhyphenated:

```
boric acid solution          hydrogen sulphide gas
sodium chloride crystals     tartaric acid powder
```

3:25 All compound adjectives indicating colour should be spelled as separate words:

```
grey green                   ruby red
dark blue                    silver grey
reddish purple               coal black
```

3:26 Compounds with *all-* should be hyphenated whether they precede or follow the noun:

```
all-encompassing aim         all-round leader
all-powerful ruler           all-inclusive title
all-out effort               the evil was all-pervasive
```

3:27 Hyphenate phrases used as adjectives before a noun:

```
six-to-ten-year-old group    matter-of-fact approach
on-the-job training          wage-price controls
catch-as-catch-can attitude  fringe-benefits demands
```

3:28 Most compounds made up of adjective plus past participles should be hyphenated before a noun and spelled as two words after a noun:

```
rosy-cheeked boy             fine-grained powder
straight-sided dish          open-handed person
```

<u>but</u>:
For a city child he was beautifully rosy cheeked

3:29 Adjective forms ending with the suffix *-like* should be spelled as one word except when they are formed from proper names, word-combinations, or words ending with *ll* (double ell):

```
barrellike                   mouselike
camplike                     umbrellalike
museumlike                   lacelike
```

<u>but</u>:
Tito-like, doll-like, kitchen-cabinet-like

3:30   An adjectival compound composed of a cardinal number and the word *-odd* should be hyphenated:

```
forty-odd               twenty-five-hundred-odd
175-odd                 fifteen-hundred-odd
```

3:31   An adjectival compound composed of a cardinal number and a unit of measurement should be hyphenated when it precedes a noun:

```
twelve-mile limit       eight-space indention
two-inch margin         100-yard dash

but:  10 per cent increase
```

3:32   Adjectival compounds with *-fold* are written as one word, unless figures are used:

```
tenfold                 multifold

but:  20-fold
```

3:33   Noun compounds with *quasi* should be spelled as two words:

```
quasi promise           quasi honour
```

Adjectival compounds with *quasi-* should be hyphenated whether they come before or after the noun:

```
quasi-religious         quasi-political
```

3:34   The trend in the spelling of compound words has for some years been away from the use of hyphens. Nowhere is this more evident than in words with such common prefixes as pre- post- pro- anti- over- under- intra- extra- infra-ultra- sub- super- re- un- non- semi- pseudo- supra-:

```
prenuptial              understaffed
postoperative           intramural
antirevolutionary       extramural
oversupplied            infrared
subatomic               ultraviolet
supersonic              semiconscious
unconcerned             supramundane
```

Adjectives with these prefixes are spelled as one word—unless the second element is capitalized or is a figure:

```
pro-Arab    un-American    pre-1900
```

or unless it is necessary to distinguish homonyms:

```
re-cover                re-create
```

or unless the second element consists of more than one word:

```
non-food-producing people
pre-nuclear-age civilization
```

DIVISION OF WORDS

GENERAL RULES

3:35 In general, divide words at the end of lines according to their syllabication as described in *Hart's Rules for Compositors and Readers*, pages 13-15. Otherwise follow a dictionary, such as the current edition of *Collins Dictionary of the English Language,* which separates the syllables with a centred dot.

3:36 In general divide according to pronunciation (rather than derivation). This means that when dividing after an accented syllable, the consonant stays with the vowel when the vowel is short:

```
signif-icant    param-eter       prej-udice
philos-ophy     hypoth-esis
```

but goes with the following syllable when it is long:

```
stu-dent        Mongo-lian    divi-sive
```

3:37 Never divide a combination of letters pronounced as one syllable:

```
pro-nounced    ex-traor-di-nary    passed
```

3:38 When *-ing* or *-ed* is added to a word whose final syllable contains the liquid *l* (e.g., *cir·cle, han·dle*), the final syllable of the parent word becomes a part of the added syllable:

```
cir-cling    bris-tling    chuck-ling    han-dling
cir-cled     bris-tled     chuck-led     han-dled
```

3:39 In words where an end consonant is doubled before *-ing* and *-ed,* the division comes between the double consonants:

```
set-ting            con-trol-ling
per-mit-ting        per-mit-ted
```

Note that this rule does not apply to words originally ending in a double consonant:

```
add-ing                 amass-ing
```

EXCEPTIONS AND SPECIAL RULES

3:40   Some divisions, although syllabically correct, should never be made.

3:41   Never make a one-letter division:

> Wrong: a-mong   u-nite   e-nough   man-y

3:42   Never divide the syllables *-able* and *-ible*:

> Wrong: inevita-ble   permissi-ble   allowa-ble
> Right: inevi-table   permis-sible   allow-able

3:43   Never divide the following suffixes:

> -cious   -geous   -cial   -cion   -sion
> -ceous   -gious   -sial   -gion   -tion
>   -tious   -tial

3:44   Avoid two-letter divisions, especially when the division would give a misleading appearance:

> Not: wo-man   of-ten   pray-er   mon-ey   loss-es

3:45   Avoid division of hyphenated words except at the hyphen:

> Not: self-evi-dent   gov-er-nor-elect   well-in-ten-tioned

3:46   Avoid division of a proper name unless it is one in which the correct division is obvious:

> Right: Wash-ing-ton   Went-worth   Bond-field   John-son

3:47   Never divide initials used in place of given names. It is best to write given names or initials on the same line as the surname, but it is allowable to place all the initials on one line and the surname on the next:

> Wrong: T./S. Eliot   J./B. S. or   J. B./S. Haldane
> Allowable: T. S./Eliot   J. B. S./Haldane

3:48   Never divide capital letters used as abbreviations for names of countries or states (U.K., U.S.A., N.Y.); or for names of organizations (YMCA, NATO); or for names of publications (*PMLA*); or radio or television stations (HTV, KKHI, KQED; but two sets of initials separated by a hyphen, e.g., KRON-FM, may be divided after the hyphen). Similarly, never divide the abbreviations for academic degrees (B.A., M.Sc., LL.D., Ph.D.).

36

3:49   Never divide a day of the month from the month, and never divide any such combinations as the following:

£6.48   A.D. 1895   6.40 p.m.   245 mi.   10%

3:50   Never end a line with a divisional mark, such as (*a*) or (1), or with a pound or a dollar sign, or an opening quotation mark, or an opening parenthesis, or an opening bracket; and never begin a line with an ending quotation mark, or an ending parenthesis, or an ending bracket, or with any mark of punctuation save only a dash (—).

3:51   For rules on the division of words in foreign languages, consult the current edition of *Hart's Rules for Compositors and Readers*.

PUNCTUATION

3:52   Punctuation in some of its specialized uses is treated elsewhere in this *Manual*, in the chapters on abbreviations, numbers, footnotes, bibliographies, quotations, tables, and illustrations. Here, the general use of the various marks of punctuation in the text is dealt with briefly, the primary aim being to provide answers to questions that frequently puzzle writers.

FULL STOP

3:53   A full stop, or period, is used at the end of a complete declarative sentence, a moderately imperative sentence, and a sentence containing an indirect question:

They took the short road into the village.

Take the short road.

The driver asked which road he should take.

3:54   A full stop denoting an abbreviation and coming at the end of a sentence may serve also as the closing full stop. If the sentence ends with a question mark or an exclamation mark, the abbreviation period is retained:

The meeting adjourned at 5.30 p.m.

Was the committee called for 8.00 p.m.?

37

How incredible that the speaker should have given
the date as 700 B.C.!

3:55   The full stop is omitted at the ends of items in a vertical list or
enumeration, whether or not the items are composed of
sentences:

1.   The securities markets

2.   The securities industry

3.   The securities industry in the economy

1.   Emphasis is on the discovery of truth

2.   Emphasis is on the useful

3.   Emphasis is on form and harmony

4.   Emphasis is on love of people, especially the
altruistic and philanthropic aspects of love

5.   Emphasis is on power, whether within or without
the narrow field of politics

6.   Emphasis is on unity

3:56   Omit full stops at the end of all the following: (1) display
headings for chapters, tables, plates, and so on; (2) any
subheading that is typed on a line by itself; (3) superscriptions
and legends; (4) boxheadings and cut-in headings in tables; (5)
address and date lines in communications, and signatures.

3:57   Full stops in series (ellipsis points) are used to mark omissions
in quoted matter (see paras. 5:16–23), and to guide the eye
(leaders) in relating items in one column of a table to relevant
items in opposite columns (see paras. 10:23, 10:26).

QUESTION MARK

3:58   A question mark is used at the end of a whole sentence
containing a query or at the end of a query making up part of
a sentence:

What has been the result of these studies?

Would the teacher-transplant idea catch on in countries other than Germany? was the question the rejects
were asking.

The question put by the Board was, Would the
taxpayers vote another bond issue that would raise
their taxes?

Note the capitalization of the first word of the sentence that
asks the question, even though it is included in another
sentence.

3:59   Courtesy disguises as a question such requests as the
following, which should end with a full stop rather than a
question mark.

Will you please submit my request to the appropriate
office.

3:60   A question mark may be used to indicate uncertainty:

The Italian painter Niccolo dell' Abbate (1512?-1571)
assisted in the decorations at Fontainebleau.

EXCLAMATION MARK

3:61   An exclamation mark is used to mark an outcry or an
emphatic or ironical comment (avoid over-use of this device).
Like the question mark, it may occur within a declarative
sentence:

What havoc was wrought by hurricane Agnes!

"Incredible!" he exclaimed, "I could hardly believe
my senses. Both Houses actually passed major Bills
on the opening day!"

"It is really too kind of you to warn me of the
slights I am about to encounter!"

"I saw my sixteen-year-old son leap to his feet--
if only I could have stopped him!--and loudly
challenge the speaker."

3:62   Do not use an exclamation mark to call attention to an error
in a quotation, but place the word *sic* enclosed in square
brackets after the error (see para. 5:40).

COMMA

3:63   Although the comma indicates the smallest interruption in
continuity of thought or sentence structure, when it is

correctly used it does more for ease of reading and ready understanding than any other mark of punctuation.

3:64   In sentences containing two independent clauses joined by a coordinating conjunction (*and, but, or, nor, for*), a comma is usually placed before the conjunction. This is not a hard-and-fast rule, however; where the sentence is short and clarity is not an issue, no comma is needed:

Most young Europeans spend their holidays in other European countries, and many students take vacation jobs abroad.

I do not think we can conclude that dissent leads to counter-revolution, but it seems certain that dissent, in itself, does not constitute a revolution.

This silence is not surprising, for in those circles Modernism is still regarded with suspicion.

but:
John arrived early and Mary came an hour later.

3:65   Do not use a comma before a conjunction joining the parts of a compound predicate (i.e., two or more verbs having the same subject):

The agencies should design their own monitoring networks and evaluate the data derived from them.

They do not self-righteously condemn such societies but attempt rather to refute them theoretically.

3:66   A series of three or more words, phrases, or clauses (like the following) takes a comma between each of the elements and before a conjunction separating the last two:

New York, Chicago, and Los Angeles were the cities mentioned.

She asserted that dishes had been broken, cutlery lost, and carpets and upholstery damaged beyond possibility of renovation.

3:67   No commas should be used, however, when the elements in a series are all joined by conjunctions:

For dessert the menu offered peaches or strawberries or melon.

3:68   A series of three or more words, phrases, or clauses ending with the expression *and so forth* or *and so on* or *and the like* or *etc.* should have commas both preceding and following the expression:

```
You can improve wages, hours, conditions, benefits,
and so on, as part of the cure.
```

```
The basket was overflowing with beans, peas, carrots,
etc., from his own garden.
```

3:69   When commas occur within one or more of the elements of a series, semicolons instead of commas should be used to separate the elements:

```
Three cities that have had notable success with the
programme are Hartford, Connecticut; Kalamazoo,
Michigan; and Pasadena, California.
```

```
The percentages of failures were as follows:
Class A, 7 per cent; Class B, 13 per cent; and
Class C, 20 per cent.
```

3:70   A comma may be used to mark an omission of a word or words made clear by the context:

```
In spring and autumn there is hiking here; in summer,
sailing; in winter, skiing.
```

Sometimes the construction is sufficiently clear without the commas as well as the semicolons (which the use of the commas makes necessary), and simpler punctuation is used:

```
Three students were from India, two from Turkey, and
eight from Japan.
```

3:71   Use commas to set off a non-restrictive clause or phrase following a main clause. An element is non-restrictive if it can be omitted without altering the meaning of the main clause:

```
These books, which are placed on reserve in the
library, are required reading for the course.
```

The clause is non-restrictive, since the meaning of the main clause, "These books are required reading for the course", is unchanged if the parenthetical clause is omitted. But in the following sentence, the clause identifies the books placed on reserve as those "that are required reading for the course", and the clause is therefore restrictive. No commas should be used:

```
The books that are required reading for the
course are placed on reserve in the library.
```

3:72   A word, phrase, or clause in apposition to a noun may also be restrictive or non-restrictive. When it is non-restrictive, it is set off by commas:

```
His brother, a Manchester graduate, transferred to
Oxford to read theology.
```

A one-time officer in the foreign legion, the man
hoped to escape further military duty.

If, however, the apposition limits the meaning of the noun
and is therefore restrictive, no commas should be used:

The Danish philosopher Kierkegaard asks, "What is
anxiety?"

The motion picture <u>Becket</u> is adapted from the play by
Jean Anouilh.

3:73   Similarly, commas are generally used to set off a phrase
indicating the place of residence, immediately following a
personal name:

Representative Sidney R. Yates, of Illinois, was the
first speaker.

Note, however, that the commas should be omitted in those
cases where the place name has practically become a part of
the person's name:

St Francis of Assisi   John of Austria

3:74   The name of a title or position following a person's name
should be set off with commas:

Norman Cousins, the former editor of the <u>Saturday</u>
<u>Review</u>, wrote the editorial "Lunar Meditations".

3:75   Set off with commas the individual elements in addresses and
names of places:

The address is 10 Upper Grosvenor Street,
London, W1X 9PA.

The next leg of our trip was to take us to Beirut,
Lebanon, and promised to be the most rewarding.

3:76   Set off with commas interjections, transitional adverbs, and
the like, when they cause a distinct break in the flow of
thought:

His statement, therefore, cannot be verified.

That, after all, is a matter of great importance.

Indeed, this is precisely what Martens feared.

It is, perhaps, the best that could be expected.

But note that when such elements do not cause a break in
continuity and do not require a pause in reading, the commas
should be omitted:

```
It is therefore clear that no deposits were made.

This is indeed the crux of the matter.

Perhaps it requires further explication.
```

3:77   In using commas to set off a parenthetical element in the middle of a sentence, the writer must remember to include both commas:

Wrong: The bill, you will be pleased to hear passed at the last session.

Right: The bill, you will be pleased to hear, passed at the last session.

Wrong: The problem of communication is less serious it is held, with the new generation than with the old.

Right: The problem of communication is less serious, it is held, with the new generation than with the old.

3:78   Use a comma following *namely, that is, for example, i.e., e.g.* There must be a punctuation mark before each of these expressions, but the kind of mark varies with the nature and complexity of the sentence:

Two other countries with a combined population of 45 million, namely, Greece and Turkey, are already half-members.

Many people feel resentful because they think they have suffered an unjust fate; that is, they look upon illness, bereavement, deranged domestic or working conditions as being undeserved.

Restrictions on the sulphur content of fuel oil are already in effect in some cities (e.g., Paris, Milan, Rome, and Stockholm), and the prospect is that limits will be imposed sooner or later in most cities.

3:79   When a dependent clause or a long participial or prepositional phrase begins a sentence, it is usually followed by a comma:

If the insurrection is to succeed, the army and the police must stand side by side.

After spending a week in conferences, the commission was able to write a report.

Because of traffic delays, the party missed the plane.

Pampering their cars, Europeans spend in the neighbourhood of 10 per cent of their income on operating and maintaining them.

Faced with the threat of a tight supply situation, European governments are casting about for solutions to the problem.

3:80 No comma should follow a participial phrase that is part of the main verb or an adverbial phrase that immediately precedes the verb it modifies. And a comma is usually unnecessary after a short prepositional phrase:

Strolling through the Temple of Athena were tourists mostly from Sweden and Denmark.

From the Olympic Tower comes greatly improved TV reception.

Beneath the Karlsplatz will be a four-level city within a city.

On Fridays we usually go to our weekend cottage.

For recreation the mayor fishes or sails.

3:81 When each of several adjectives preceding a noun modifies the noun individually, they should be separated with commas:

It was a large, well-placed, beautiful house.

We stroll out into the warm, luminous night.

However, if the last adjective *identifies* the noun rather than merely modifying it, no comma should precede it:

Then in the procession came the tall, dignified third-year students.

His is the large brick house on the corner.

3:82 Set off with commas contrasted elements and two or more complementary or antithetical phrases or clauses referring to a single word following:

The idea, not its expression, is significant.

The harder we run, the more we stay in the same place.

She both delighted in, and was disturbed by, her new leisure and freedom.

It is a logical, if a harsh, solution to the problem.

44

3:83   Use a comma to separate two identical or closely similar words:

They marched in, in twos.

Whatever is, had best be accepted.

3:84   A comma should be used to prevent misreading of such sentences as the following:

From the British, educated Indians learned the principles of parliamentary democracy.

After eating, the lions yawned and then dozed.

SEMICOLON

3:85   A semicolon marks a greater break in the continuity of a sentence than that indicated by a comma. Use a semicolon between the parts of a compound sentence (two or more independent clauses) when they are not connected by a conjunction:

More than one hundred planned communities are in various stages of completion; many more are on the drawing boards.

3:86   If the clauses of a compound sentence are very long and there are commas within them, they should be separated with semicolons even though they are connected by a conjunction:

Although productivity per man in U.S. industry is almost twice that in West European industry, Western Europe has an increasingly well-educated young labour force; and the crucial point is that knowledge, which is transferable between peoples, has become by far the most important world economic resource.

3:87   When used transitionally between the clauses of compound sentences, the words *hence, however, indeed, so, then, thus,* and *yet* are considered adverbs, not conjunctions, and should therefore be preceded by semicolons rather than commas:

There are those who consider freedom basically in terms of social and economic egalitarianism; thus, reformist governments of the left are inherently viewed with greater favour than the status-quo regimes of the right.

> The idea of a "cultural army" goes far back in Mao's
> works; however, he is not innovating: culture is
> always the reflection of political and social reality.

3:88   For the use of a semicolon instead of a comma, see
paragraphs 3:69–70, 3:78.

COLON

3:89   The use of the colon in a sentence indicates a discontinuity of
grammatical construction greater than that indicated by the
semicolon. Whereas the semicolon is used to separate parts
that are usually of equal significance, the colon is used to
introduce a clause or phrase that expands, clarifies, or
exemplifies the meaning of what precedes it:

> The New World and the Old share the same monumental
> urban problems: their populations mount, and in all
> industrial nations the migration from country to city
> has become a flood.

> People at present seek three main things through and
> partly from their governmental systems: peace,
> prosperity, and a more cohesively gracious form of
> living together.

3:90   A colon should be placed at the end of a grammatical element
introducing a formal statement, whether the statement is
quoted or not. It is usually placed after *following* or *as
follows* or *in sum* when the enumerated items or illustrations
come immediately after:

> His "laws" are as follows:
> 1.   Books are for use
> 2.   For every reader his book
> 3.   For every book its reader

3:91   As noted elsewhere in this *Manual*, a colon is used between
chapter and verse in scriptural references (para. 2:11), and
between place and publisher in footnote and bibliographical
references (para. 6:54).

DASH

3:92   The dash, which in printing is a continuous line, in typescript consists of two hyphens without space between or on either side of them. It should be used sparingly.

3:93   A dash or a pair of dashes may indicate a sudden break in thought that disrupts the sentence structure:

The characters in Tom Jones tend to be "flat"--
to use the term E. M. Forster made fashionable--
because there is often little or no sign of conflict.

To this the young man answered--he must have been
very young--"I will do as you say."

3:94   Breaks in faltering speech or interruptions should be indicated by dashes:

"Well, it's as I said, difficult to explain--but
the service, being considered so important by us
Russians--if you were absent--I don't know how to
put it, people might think--might think--"

Becky and Ann--where have they gone?

3:95   Use a dash to introduce an element that emphasizes or explains the main clause through repetition of a key word or key words:

He asked where wisdom was to be found--"the wisdom
that is above rubies".

One is expected to cram all this stuff into one's
mind--cram it all in, whether it's likely to be
useful or not.

3:96   In a sentence that includes several elements referring to a word that is the subject of a final, summarizing clause, a dash should precede the final clause:

The statue of the man throwing the discus, the
charioteer at Delphi, the poetry of Pindar--all
show the culmination of the great ideal.

3:97   A word or phrase set on a line by itself, the meaning of which is completed by two or more parallel elements that follow, may end with a dash:

On two major propositions the consensus was--
1. that the historical function of the library
    has been as an agency of culture;

2.   that the selective initial dissemination of
     published material is a direct responsibility
     of libraries.

When such parallel elements are run into the text, no dash is used:

On two major propositions the consensus was (1) that
the historical function of the library has been as
an agency of culture, and (2) that the selective
initial dissemination of published material is a
direct responsibility of libraries.

For the use of numbers to enumerate items in text, see paragraph 2:55.

PARENTHESES

3:98   The principal uses of parentheses in the text of a paper are (1) to set off parenthetical elements, (2) to enclose the source of a quotation or other matter when a footnote is not used for the purpose, and (3) to set off the numbers or letters in an enumeration (like that in this sentence). The first use is a matter of choice, since both commas and dashes are also used to set off parenthetical material. In general, commas are used for material most closely related to the main clause, dashes and parentheses for material more remotely connected. The following examples illustrate some instances where parentheses might be used:

The conference has (with some malice aforethought)
been divided into four major areas.

It is significant that in the book of Revelation
(a book Whitehead did not like because of its bloody
and apocalyptic imagery) the vision of a new heavenly
city at the end of time has the divine light shine so
that the nations walk by it, and the "kings of the
earth shall bring their glory into it" (Rev. 21:22-26).

SQUARE BRACKETS

3:99   Square brackets are used (1) to enclose any interpolation in a quotation (see paras. 5:39–41) and (2) to enclose parenthetical matter within a parenthesis:

> The book is available in translation (see J. R. Evans-
> Wentz, <u>The Tibetan Book of the Dead</u> [Oxford: Oxford
> University Press, 1927]).

3:100 If within the bracket further parenthesis is required, use parentheses again:

> The various arguments advanced (these include certain
> anonymous writers [<u>Public Economy</u> (New York, 1848)])
> may be formulated thus: . . .

OTHER PUNCTUATION MARKS

3:101 The use of quotation marks is described in paragraphs 5:9–14.

3:102 The hyphen, sometimes considered a mark of punctuation, is discussed in paragraphs 3:12–51 (compound words and word division) and paragraph 2:52 (continued numbers).

MULTIPLE PUNCTUATION

3:103 The term *multiple punctuation* means the conjunction of two marks of punctuation—for example, a full stop and a closing parenthesis. Where such conjunction occurs, certain rules must be observed concerning (1) whether to omit one mark or the other (as a full stop when an abbreviation ends a sentence, see para. 3:54) or (2) which mark to put first when both marks are kept.

3:104 A comma is generally omitted following a stronger mark of punctuation:

> If he had consulted <u>Who Was When?</u> he would have found
> the answer.

> The owner yelled, "Get out!" and the robber fled.

3:105 The comma is retained after the dash in certain special instances, and always when it falls after an abbreviation with a full stop.

> "If you were absent—I don't know how to put it—
> people might think—might think—," Vasily finished on
> a rising note of inquiry.

Never use the contractions St, Ave, or Rd in formal correspondence.

3:106 Two marks of punctuation fall in the same place chiefly where quotation marks, parentheses, or brackets are involved.

3:107 In British usage, with quotation marks, a final comma or full stop goes outside (i.e. after the closing quotation mark) unless it is part of the quoted matter. (In American usage, with quotation marks, a final comma or full stop always goes *inside*, i.e., before the closing quotation mark, whether it is part of the quoted matter or not.) Question marks and exclamation points go inside if they are part of the quoted matter, outside if they pertain to the entire sentence of which the quotation is a part. Semicolons and colons go outside the quotation marks, as part of the sentence containing the quotation. (If the quoted passage ends with a semicolon or a colon in the original, the mark would normally be changed to a period or a comma to accord with the structure of the main sentence.)

Every public official and every professional person is called upon "to join in the effort to bring justice and hope to all our people".

The probable is not what accords with some hypothesis about the "existing laws of human affairs", nor is it what accords with the "ordinary processes of life".

Even this small advance begins to raise the question, "What in effect is our true image, our real likeness?"

Thus a novel is not analysed, . . . until we have discovered its place in the mind of the novelist (is this the "intentional fallacy"?), in the movement of the age.

Do we accept Jefferson's concept of "a natural aristocracy among men"?

Charged by a neighbour with criminal mistreatment of her child and threatened with police action, the woman retorted, "You call the police, and you'll regret it to your dying day!"

How dreadful it was to hear her reply--calmly--"We'll let the law decide that"!

He made the point that "in every human attitude and choice we make, we are taking an attitude toward

Everyman"; and then enlarged upon the point in a
particularly telling way.

Rome's one planned subcentre, EUR, is "almost a self-
contained city": it governs itself and provides its
own services.

3:108   In fields where it is the practice to use single quotation marks
to set off special terms, a full stop or comma follows the
closing quotation mark:

Some contemporary theologians were proclaiming the
'death of God'.

But in the following title of an article which includes the title
of another article, the full stop is correctly placed within the
closing quotation marks, both single and double:

The article to which he referred is in the Journal
of Political Economy: "Comment on 'How to Make a
Burden of the Public Debt'."

3:109   When a complete sentence enclosed in parentheses or brackets
stands alone, the full stop for that sentence is placed within
the parentheses or brackets. When the parenthetical sentence
appears inside another sentence, however, the full stop is
omitted:

We have already noted similar motifs in Japan.
(Significantly, very similar motifs can also be
found in the myths and folk tales of Korea.)

The car crept up the driveway (I saw it turn in
from the road) and paused just short of the entrance.

3:110   No punctuation should be placed between a parenthetical
element and the element it modifies or to which it is closely
connected.   Therefore,   internal   sentence   punctuation
normally   follows   the   parenthetical   element   and   no
punctuation precedes it:

Myths have been accepted as literally true, then
as allegorically true (by the Stoics), as confused
history (by Euhemerus), as priestly lies (by the
philosophers of the Enlightenment), as imitative
agricultural ritual mistaken for propositions (in
the days of Frazer).

"If he [the believer] stops here [with the base
statement of election with reference only to himself],
who shall blame him?"

51

Stephen Enke, <u>Economics for Development</u> (Englewood Cliffs, N.J.: <u>Prentice-Hall, 1963</u>), p. 91.

Madrid received via Brussels not only its correspondence from England (the most important focus of Spanish diplomacy in the period), northern Europe, and the emperor, but often even the dispatches from Rome.

It is clear that one of the main motives was to reduce the speaking roles (even as a new role, that of the Clown, was being built up); and the action has been padded in several places.

Deep underground here, a "forum" will be built (like the galleries of Naples and Milan): elegant stores, cinemas, and restaurants as fine as any of their Italian counterparts.

3:111   Numbers or letters in an enumeration in the text belong with the items following them, and therefore sentence punctuation precedes them and no punctuation mark comes between them and the item to which they apply:

He gave three reasons for resigning: (1) advanced age, (2) failing health, and (3) a desire to travel.

3:112   Square brackets used to set off words or phrases supplied to fill in incomplete parts of a quotation (para. 5:39) or dates supplied in citations (para. 6:67) are ignored in punctuating—i.e., punctuate as if there were no brackets:

The states have continued to respond to "the federal stimulus for improvement in the scope and amount of categorical assistance programs. . . . [Yet] Congress has adhered to its original decision that residence requirements were necessary."

New York: Macmillan Co., [1910]

4 Capitalization, Underlining, and Other Matters of Style

CAPITALIZATION

PROPER NAMES

4:1 In all languages written in the Latin alphabet proper nouns (the names of persons and places) are capitalized:

`John and Jane Doe`   `Niagara Falls`

4:2 In English, proper adjectives (adjectives derived from proper nouns) are also capitalized:

`European`   `Machiavellian`

4:3 But proper nouns and adjectives that have lost their original meanings and become part of everyday language are not capitalized:

`french doors`   `indian ink`

OTHER NAMES

4:4 Except for proper names the practice of capitalization varies widely. Names of organizations and political divisions are usually capitalized, but not always. Titles of persons are sometimes capitalized but by no means always. In modern usage the tendency is wherever possible *not* to capitalize. The writer of a paper should decide, before the final typescript is prepared, which terms are to be capitalized and which are not. Inconsistency in the matter is a sign of sloppy writing. Detailed suggestions for capitalization of many terms occurring in the run of text may be found in *Hart's Rules for*

53

Compositors and Readers. The following paragraphs discuss the capitalization of titles of written works, the problem encountered most frequently by writers of papers.

TITLES OF WORKS

4:5 In giving titles of published works in text, footnotes, or bibliography, the spelling of the original should be retained, but capitalization and punctuation may be altered to conform to the style used in the paper. In most scientific fields capitalization is kept to a minimum (see chapter 12 for examples). In the humanities and most of the social sciences, however, it is customary to capitalize titles according to the rules given in the following paragraphs.

4:6 In the titles of English works, capitalize the first and last words and all words except articles, prepositions, and coordinate conjunctions:

<u>Economic Effects of the War upon Women and Children</u>

"What It Is All About"

<u>How to Overcome Urban Blight: A Twentieth-Century Problem</u>

Note that the subtitle, following a colon, is capitalized in the same way as the main title.

4:7 Rules for capitalizing compound words vary widely. In general, capitalize both elements of a compound word that is hyphenated for syntactical reasons, such as *Twentieth-Century* when used as an adjective as in the last example in para. 4:6; capitalize only the first element of a compound word that is a separate word in its own right, such as *Self-sustaining, Mother-in-law.*

4:8 The original capitalization of long titles of works published in earlier centuries is usually retained:

<u>The precedents of general issues, and the most usual special pleas; precedents of replications, rejoinders, demurrers, &c; a synopsis of practice, or general view of the time when the proceedings in an action should be carried on in the Court of King's Bench and Common Pleas.</u>

4:9   In the titles of French, Italian, and Spanish works, capitalize the first word and proper nouns:

Dictionnaire illustré de la mythologie et des
antiquités grecques et romaines

Bibliografia di Roma nel' Cinquecento

Historia de la Orden de San Gerónimo

4:10   In German titles, capitalize the first word and all nouns, both common and proper, but not proper adjectives:

Reallexikon zur deutschen Kunstgeschichte

4:11   In Greek and Latin titles, capitalize the first word and proper nouns and proper adjectives:

Iphigeneia hē en Taurois

Speculum Romanae magnificentiae

4:12   An exception is made for modern works with Latin titles, which usually are capitalized as though they were English:

Acta Apostolicae Sedis   Quo Vadis?

4:13   Such parts of a work as *contents, preface, foreword, introduction, bibliography, appendix* should not be capitalized in passing references:

A foreword may be included if desired.

The paper should include a bibliography.

But when references are made to a *specific work,* the name of the part is capitalized or not, in accordance with the rule in paragraphs 4:14 and 4:15 below.

4:14   When the reference is made to a part of which there is but one in the work (e.g., Preface, Table of Contents, Bibliography), the name of that part is capitalized:

The Preface to this popular work was written by
Lionel Trilling.

The Table of Contents lists only chapter numbers
and titles.

The Bibliography is classified into works by the
author and works about the author.

4:15   But when the reference is to a part of which there is more than one, such as chapters, parts, figures, tables, the name of the part is not capitalized:

```
"Thinking French" is the title of chapter 6.

The physical conditions of the experiment are
listed in table 2.

Copies of supporting documents are in appendix 3.
```

If there was but *one* appendix, the word would be capitalized:

```
The Appendix contains the supporting documents.
```

UNDERLINING AND QUOTATION MARKS FOR TITLES

4:16   In all fields except some of the sciences, some titles of written works, published or unpublished, and some other kinds of names and titles are underlined (to indicate a title that would be italicized in printing); others are enclosed in double quotation marks, and still others are capitalized but neither underlined nor enclosed in quotation marks. The general rule is to underline the titles of *whole* published works and to put the titles of *parts of* these works in quotation marks. Titles of unpublished material are also in quotation marks. Titles of series and manuscript collections, and various kinds of descriptive titles, are neither underlined nor in quotation marks.

BOOKS AND PERIODICALS

4:17   Underline the titles of books, pamphlets, bulletins, periodicals (magazines, journals, newspapers). It should be noted that although a published work is usually thought of as set in type and printed in conventional form, it may be a typewritten script reproduced by a whole range of reprographic processes, including microfilming (see para. 6:118). *If the work bears a publisher's imprint,* it should be treated as published rather than unpublished material; that is, the title should be underlined wherever it is referred to.

4:18   Titles of chapters or other titled divisions of a book, short stories and essays, and articles in periodicals are set in quotation marks.

The First Circle, chap. 27, "A Puzzled Robot"

"The New Feminism", Saturday Review

"Amazing Amazon Region", New York Times

"The Demon Lover", Fifty Years: A Retrospective Collection . . .

Part 4 of the Systematic Theology, "Life and the Spirit"

BOOK SERIES AND EDITIONS

4:19   Titles of series and names of editions are neither underlined nor put in quotation marks:

The Soho Bibliographies
Oxford English Novels
New Penguin Shakespeare

DISSERTATIONS AND PAPERS

4:20   Titles of unpublished theses and dissertations and other papers are set in quotation marks:

"Intergenerational Family Helping Patterns" (Ph.D. dissertation, University of Minnesota, 1964)

"Costing of Human Resource Development", paper presented at the Conference of the International Economics Association

"One Man's CBI: A Different Kind of War", unpublished MSS, Hoover Library, Stanford, Calif.

MANUSCRIPT COLLECTIONS

4:21   Names of manuscript collections and archives and designations such as *diary, memorandum,* etc., are not underlined or set in quotation marks:

British Museum, Harleian MSS

Hoover Library, Stanford, California, unpublished MSS

See also paras. 6:119–20.

SACRED SCRIPTURE

4:22 The titles of books of sacred scripture (Bible, Koran, Talmud, Upanishads, Vedas, etc.) and the names of books of the Bible and of the Apocrypha are neither underlined nor set in quotation marks:

the King James Version of the Bible

The Book of Daniel is a part of the apocalyptic literature of the Bible.

POEMS

4:23 Titles of long poems are underlined: titles of short poems are in quotation marks:

Milton's Paradise Lost

"Pied Beauty", in The Oxford Book of Modern Verse

PLAYS AND FILMS

4:24 Titles of plays and films are underlined:

O'Neill's The Iceman Cometh

the film Citizen Kane

RADIO AND TELEVISION PROGRAMMES

4:25 Titles of radio and television programmes are set in quotation marks:

ITV's "News at Ten"

BBC's "Panorama"

MUSICAL COMPOSITIONS

4:26 Actual titles of long musical compositions (operas, oratorios, symphonies, ballets, tone poems) are underlined; titles of short compositions (songs, piano pieces, and the like) are set in quotation marks:

Mozart's The Magic Flute

Handel's Messiah [not The Messiah]

Beethoven's Eroica symphony; or Symphony no. 3 (Eroica)

Stravinsky's ballet The Rite of Spring

Sibelius's tone poem Finlandia

the song "My Robin Is to the Greenwood Gone"

"Belle Nuit", from Les Contes d'Hoffmann

4:27 Many musical compositions have no title as such but are identified by the name of the musical form and the key and sometimes the number. Such designations are neither underlined nor in quotation marks. When an attributed title is given as well, it is put in quotation marks and parentheses after the designation of form and key:

Beethoven's Sonata in D Major, op. 128

Bach's Prelude and Fugue in E flat ("St Anne")

ART WORKS

4:28 Actual titles of paintings, drawings, and sculpture are underlined. Purely descriptive, or attributed, titles are not.

Rembrandt's etching Abraham's Sacrifice

van Gogh's painting The Harvest

Bernini's sculpture Apollo and Daphne

but:

Mona Lisa

Victory of Samothrace

SHIPS AND AIRCRAFT

4:29 Actual names of ships, aircraft and spacecraft are underlined. Designations of make, etc., are not:

S.S. Constitution	Spirit of St Louis
H.M.S. Saranac	Apollo XIII

59

FOREIGN WORDS AND PHRASES

4:30   Underline foreign words and phrases that are used in English text without quotation marks:

> Clearly, this . . . leads to the idea of Übermensch and also to the theory of the acte gratuit and surrealism.

See also para. 4:34.

4:31   A quotation entirely in a foreign language is not underlined. In the following sentence, the words *le pragmatisme* are underlined within the English text, but the words of the quotation, all in French, are properly not underlined:

> The confusion of le pragmatisme is traced to the supposed failure to distinguish "les propriétés de la valeur en général" from the incidental.

4:32   In the following quotation, the writer has underlined some words used as examples. The person using the quotation in English text must observe the author's usage, since a quotation must always be reproduced exactly as it appears in the original:

> Reviewing Mr Wright's book, Professor Nichols writes: "Quand j'ai dû analyser le style de Wright . . . j'ai été frappé par l'emploi ironique de ses conjonctions causales (à cause, parce que, etc.)."

4:33   Foreign titles preceding proper names, and foreign names of persons, places, institutions, and the like, are not underlined:

Père Grou	the Puerto del Sol
M. Jacquet, Ministre	the Vienna Staatsoper
de Travaux	the Quai d'Orsay
the Académie Française	the Gare du Nord
the Teatro real	the Casa de los Guzmanes

4:34   Do not underline in English text those foreign words which by continued use in English have become anglicized. Listed below are some of the more common anglicized words. Note that some words in the list do not show the accent marks proper to their native forms. In others the accent marks are retained and must be inserted in ink, by hand, unless your typewriter has them. It is never permissible to use an apostrophe for a grave or an acute accent mark; it is permissible, however, to use a comma for a cedilla and quotation marks for an umlaut.

a posteriori	kapellmeister
a priori	laissez faire
ad hoc	mea culpa
ad infinitum	mélange
ante bellum	ménage
apropos	milieu
attaché	mores
barranca	naïveté
beau idéal	par excellence
bête noire	pasha
blitzkrieg	per annum
bona fide	per capita
bourgeoisie	per cent
café	per se
carte blanche	précis
chargé d'affaires	pro rata
cliché	rapport
clientele	rapprochement
communiqué	recherché
contretemps	regime
coup d'état	remuda
coup de grâce	résumé
debris	role
dénouement	status quo
de rigueur	subpoena
dilettante	tête-à-tête
doyen	Übermensch
élan	versus
émigré	via
entrée	vice versa
entrepreneur	vis-à-vis
ex officio	visa
exposé	Weltanschauung
façade	Weltschmerz
genre	
habeas corpus	

4:35   In general, foreign words and expressions not included in the foregoing list should be underlined.

5   Quotations

5:1   In general, direct quotations should correspond exactly with the originals in wording, spelling, capitalization, and punctuation. Exceptions to the general rule are discussed under "Ellipses" (paras. 5:16–38). "Interpolations" (paras. 5:39–41), and "Italics" (para. 5:42).

PROSE

5:2   Short, direct prose quotations should be incorporated into the text of the paper and enclosed in double quotation marks. But in general a prose quotation of two or more sentences which at the same time runs to four or more typewritten lines should be set off from the text in single spacing and indented in its entirety four spaces from the left marginal line, with no quotation marks at beginning or end. A quotation so treated is called a *block quotation* in this *Manual*. Exceptions to this rule are allowable when, for purposes of emphasis or of comparison, it is desirable to block quotations of less than four typewritten lines in length. Paragraph indention in the original text should be indicated by a four-space indention. (See sample pages, para. 13:42.) Double-space between the text and the block quotation, but single-space between the paragraphs of the quotation, except when quoting passages from different works of the same author, or from different authors, in which cases double-space between the separate passages.

POETRY

5:3   Quotations of poetry two or more lines in length should normally be set off from the text, line for line as in the original, single-spaced, and centred on the page:

```
                    The river sweats
                    Oil and tar
                    The barges drift
                    With the turning tide
                    Red sails
                    Wide
                    To leeward, swing on the heavy spar.
                        T. S. Eliot, "The Waste Land"
```

5:4   If the lines of the poem are too long to be centred on the page, all the lines should be indented four spaces, with any runover lines indented another four spaces:

```
                    The yellow bird sings in their tree and
                        makes my heart dance with gladness.
                    We both live in the same village, and
                        that is our one piece of joy.
                                Rabindranath Tagore,
                                "The Yellow Bird Sings"
```

5:5   In quoting excerpts of poems, as shown above, use no quotation marks at beginning and end. Use quotation marks, however, when giving successive quotations from poems by the same author or by different authors; place quotation marks at the beginning of every stanza and at the end of only the last. Leave an extra space between poems of the same author, and between excerpts from different authors.

5:6   It is sometimes desirable to insert a line or two of verse directly into text. For example, a writer who is making a critical examination of a poem may find this method of quoting well suited to his purpose. Quotation marks are placed at the beginning and the end of the line or lines quoted, and, if there is more than one line, a slash (/) is used to separate them:

```
In the valley the mariners find life's purposes
reduced to the simple naturalistic proposition,
"All things have rest, and ripen toward the
grave; / In silence, ripen, fall, and cease."
```

EPIGRAPHS

5:7   When used at the heads of chapters, epigraphs are given the same indention as the paragraphs of the paper, and they are

not enclosed in quotation marks. The source is given below
the epigraph and is aligned to end with it at the right margin.

> A storm of mosquitoes may create a noise
> like thunder.
>
> Old Chinese saying

QUOTATIONS IN FOOTNOTES

5:8   Whether run in the body of the footnote or indented and set
off from it, all quoted matter appearing in footnotes is
enclosed in quotation marks:

> [1]"He leaves a terrible blank behind him and I
> have a horrid lonely feeling knowing that he is gone"
> (Field-Marshal Lord Alanbrooke, Diary, 18 April 1940
> [MS, Personal Files]). Writing of Dill somewhat later,
> Brooke expressed a strong feeling of admiration and
> affection:
>> "I know of no other soldier in the whole of my
>> career who inspired me with greater admiration
>> and respect. An exceptionally clear, well-balanced
>> brain, an infinite capacity for work, unbounded
>> charm of personality, but, above all, an
>> unflinching straightness of character . . . I owe
>> him an infinite debt for all I learned from him"
> (idem, "Notes on My Life" [MS, Personal Files],
> vol. II, p. 66).

QUOTATION MARKS

5:9   Direct quotations other than block quotations as described in
paragraphs 5:2–4 require double quotation marks at
beginning and end. If the quoted passage itself contains a
quotation that is set off with double quotation marks, those
marks must be changed to single (see para. 5:14). In a block
quotation, however, where no marks are used at beginning
and end, the double quotation marks that appear within the
original matter are retained.

5:10   In addition to their use with quotations from other sources,
double quotation marks are used to set off titles (see paras.
4:16–27) and single words, letters, or numbers in certain
contexts:

```
Twenty-one papers were prepared under the topics
"Background", "Relation to Card Catalogues", "Tech-
niques", "Standards", "Applications".

The enumerations may be either numbered "1", "2",
"3", etc., or lettered "a", "b", "c", etc.
```

In some fields, linguistics and theology for example, it is accepted practice to use single quotation marks to set off words and concepts being discussed:

```
kami 'hair, beard'
The variables of quantification, 'something',
'nothing', . . .
```

See also para. 3:108.

5:11 In quoting a letter (correspondence), quotation marks are placed at the beginning of each element of the address, of the salutation, of each paragraph, of the complimentary close, and of the signature. Closing quotation marks appear only after the signature:[1]

```
                            "Baltimore, Maryland
                            "June 1, 1965

"The University of Chicago
"Chicago, Illinois

"Gentlemen:

"Will you kindly refer my request for information
concerning the next series of public lectures on
Far Eastern art to the proper office.

                            "Very truly yours,

                            "Clyde L. Brown"
```

5:12 Similarly, in quoting an outline or an enumeration, quotation marks are placed before each unit and at the end of only the last:

```
Their outline for the third-year course is as follows:
"III.   Predicate-element concept
```

[1]The use of quotation marks as directed here and in paragraphs 5:12 and 5:13 does not reverse the rule given in paragraph 5:2, which calls for the indention and single-spacing of long quotations and the omission of quotation marks at beginning and end. But when a paper includes the writer's own outlines or similar material, single-spaced and indented, as well as the same kind of materials quoted from other writers, it is advisable to enclose all quoted matter in quotation marks.

```
"A.  Verb
    "1.  Forms and uses of verb 'to be'
    "2.  Tense
        "a)  Present perfect
        "b)  Past perfect"
```

And for an enumeration in which the items are treated as paragraphs, note the following:

```
"1.  Book selection
"2.  Arrangement and organization of the collection
"3.  Guidance to readers"
```

5:13 For a quotation that includes headings and subheadings, quotation marks are placed before each heading and subheading as well as before each paragraph, with the closing quotation marks coming only at the end of the part quoted:

"CHAPTER II

"THE DEVELOPMENT OF A RACE RELATIONS

ACTION-STRUCTURE

"Race Relations in the British
Isles: 1700 to the First World War

"From the defeat of the Spanish Armada in 1588 until the abolition of slavery throughout the British Empire in 1833, the economy of Britain was tied, in some measure, to the fortunes of the African slave trade . . .
    "There were individuals among both the adherents of Conservative and Liberal-humanitarian ideological systems who felt that, . . ."

5:14 For a quotation within a quotation, single quotation marks are used; for another quotation within that one, double marks are again used; if yet another, single marks, and so on:

The chairman reported as follows: "The mayor's representative has replied: 'I am authorized by the Chamber of Commerce to make this offer, their provision stating, "The jobs shall be made available provided that the committee guarantee all the means for receiving applications." That guarantee has been made and a procedure outlined for taking job applications.' Our thanks go to the mayor for his handling of our committee's request."

PUNCTUATION WITH QUOTATION MARKS

5:15   Full stops and commas should be placed inside quotation marks (even when the quotation marks enclose only one letter or figure); semicolons and colons, outside. Question marks and exclamation marks should be placed outside the quotation marks unless the question or the exclamation occurs within the quotation itself. In the first example below, the question is not posed within the quotation but in the sentence as a whole, and the question mark properly belongs after the closing quotation mark. In the other two examples, the question mark in one and the exclamation mark in the other clearly belong within the quotations:

Does he precisely show "evil leading somehow to good"?

One may well ask: "Is it really necessary to lose the world in order to find ourselves?"

The cries of "Long live the king!" echoed down the broad avenues.

See also paras. 3:107–8, 5:28–29.

MARKS OF OMISSION (ELLIPSES)

5:16   Any omission of words, phrases, or paragraphs in quoted matter is indicated by ellipsis points, which are dots not asterisks (stars). There should be a space before each dot, unless the first dot is a period, and a space also after the last if a word follows. Since ellipsis points stand for words omitted from the quotation itself, they are always placed *within* the quotation marks.

OMISSION WITHIN A SENTENCE

5:17   An omission within a sentence is shown by three spaced dots:

In conclusion he stated: "What we require to be taught . . . is to be our own teachers."

5:18   If other punctuation comes immediately before the ellipsis, it is placed next to the word:

"We are fighting for the holy cause of Slavdom, . . . for freedom, . . . for the Orthodox cross."

67

5:19   If other punctuation occurs immediately before a word that is preceded by ellipsis points, that punctuation mark is placed before the word, with the usual intervening space:

> "All this is not exactly in S's tradition . . .; and it was not, as I recall, your style."

OMISSION FOLLOWING A SENTENCE

5:20   An omission following a sentence is indicated by four dots. The first, placed immediately after the last word, is the full stop:

> "When a nation is clearly in the wrong, it ought not to be too proud to say so. . . . I have not been enunciating principles which we do not apply in our own case."

If in the original source the sentence preceding the ellipsis ends with a question mark or an exclamation mark, that mark rather than the full stop is used:

> "How cold it was! . . . No one could function in that climate."

5:21   How much of an omission may be indicated by a mark of terminal punctuation and three dots? In a few instances a full line of ellipsis points is used to mark the omission of a paragraph or more in a quotation set in block form. These are discussed below in paragraphs 5:22, 5:23, and 5:37. In current practice, the full stop (or other mark of terminal punctuation) and three spaced dots may indicate the omission of (1) the last part of a quoted sentence, or (2) the first part of a quoted sentence, or (3) the last part of one sentence and the first part of the next sentence, or (4) a whole sentence or more, or (5) a whole paragraph or more. But note the following exceptions.

WHEN TO USE A LINE OF ELLIPSIS POINTS

5:22   In quoting an excerpt of poetry, the omission of one or more complete lines is shown by a full line of ellipsis points, approximating in length the line of poetry immediately above it:

```
Hark! hark! the sweet vibrating lyre
Sets my attentive soul on fire;
. . . . . . . . . . . . . .
And the more slow and solemn bass
Adds charm to charm and grace to grace.
```

5:23   The use of a full line of ellipsis points may be desirable in quoting portions of an outline or an enumeration. In the following example, the four dots at the end of the first paragraph indicate both the omission of the last part of the item and of items 2 and 3. The semicolon and the three dots at the end of item 4 indicate the omission of the last part of the paragraph. The full line of dots that follows is necessary to indicate that the enumeration continues beyond the point quoted:

```
"1.  The paper must include a discussion of the
     moral bases and social effects of the kind of
     ownership which you favour or which you wish
     to attack. . . .
"4.  In form, the paper must be an argument; . . .
     . . . . . . . . . . . . . . . . . . . . . "
```

See also para. 5:38.

CAPITALIZATION OF FIRST WORD

5:24   It has been pointed out (para. 5:1) that exact quotations should follow precisely the wording, spelling, capitalization, and punctuation of the original. But long-established scholarly practice makes an exception by altering the capitalization of the first word of a quotation according to the following rule: (1) If the text matter introducing the quotation ends either with terminal punctuation or with a colon, the first word of the quotation is capitalized, even though it is not capitalized in the original:

```
The following day Sand reported: "With Pebble
soliciting members on the side, it was imperative
that the meeting be no longer delayed." [In the
original, "With" occurred inside a sentence and was
therefore not capitalized.]
```

(2) If, however, the quotation is joined syntactically to the writer's introductory words, the first word of the quotation is begun with a small letter, although it may be capitalized in the original:

```
The Act provided that "the General Council of the
Board shall exercise general supervision". [In the
original, "the" was the first word of the sentence
and was therefore capitalized.]
```

5:25   Although the practice of thus altering capitalization of the first word of a quotation is followed by many writers, there are others who hold that both the integrity of the original and ease in locating the quotation demand the use of ellipsis dots before the first word when it occurs within a sentence and the retaining of the small letter as in the original. They would write:

```
The following day Sand reported: ". . . with Pebble
soliciting members on the side, it was imperative
that the meeting be no longer delayed".
```

And when the quotation begins in the original with a capitalized word, they would retain the original capitalization, even though the quotation is joined syntactically to the writer's introductory words:

```
The Act provided that "The General Council of the
Board shall exercise general supervision".
```

TERMINAL PUNCTUATION OR ELLIPSIS POINTS?

5:26   Opinion differs concerning the use of ellipsis points at the end of a quotation.

5:27   There should be no question that when a quotation ends with the author's complete sentence, his mark of terminal punctuation and the closing quotation mark are sufficient.

5:28   According to some highly regarded opinion, terminal punctuation with the quotation mark is suitable as well either when the quoted matter is *functionally* a sentence, even though it ends with a weak mark of punctuation, or when the quoted matter combined with the writer's introductory words forms a functional sentence. In the original matter, the following quotation ended with a semicolon. Since functionally it is a sentence, some writers would place a full stop before the final quotation mark:

> "Part of the historical problem concerns the state of affairs in Spain in the period, and part concerns the state of affairs in the Spanish Netherlands."

5:29 Other reputable opinion maintains that in either of the instances set forth above, when the quoted matter forms only a part of the original sentence, the punctuation should indicate that fact by ending the quotation with the author's mark of punctuation, if there is any, plus three ellipsis points, or with the three points alone, followed by quotation marks:

> "Part of the historical problem concerns the state of affairs in Spain in the period, and part concerns the state of affairs in the Spanish Netherlands; . . ."

5:30 Choose one of the schemes set forth in paragraphs 5:28 and 5:29 and follow it consistently.

INCOMPLETE QUOTED EXPRESSIONS

5:31 When a quotation consists of a few words or an incomplete sentence, obviously a fragment from the original, no ellipsis points should be used either before or after the fragment. If, however, an omission occurs within the fragment, it is noted by three ellipsis points:

> General Bliss wrote that the president had been "very much impressed" by the South African Jan Smuts's paper which stressed "putting a considerable part of the world under tutelage . . . of the great powers".

OMISSIONS IN FOREIGN-LANGUAGE QUOTATIONS

5:32 Omissions in foreign-language quotations are treated in the same way as those in English.

BLOCK QUOTATIONS

5:33   When a block quotation (para. 5:2) begins with a paragraph in the original matter, it is given paragraph indention of four spaces and the first word is capitalized. Thus with a block quotation indented four spaces from the text, the paragraph indention is eight spaces from the text.

> Goodenough raises questions that Kraeling does not raise:
>> Primarily why did the artist want to put David as the tamer just here? We have seen that the original vine or tree growing from the vase was changed to make more explicit the symbolic and ritualistic implications of the vase.

5:34   When a quotation begins within the first sentence of a paragraph, whether or not the quotation is syntactically joined to the introductory text, the omission of the first words of the paragraph is shown by three ellipsis dots, the first dot given paragraph indention:

> We may find statements in talmudic literature which are relevant to the art, but we must in any case after assembling the material determine
>> . . . what this art means in itself, before we begin to apply to it as proof texts any possible unrelated statements of the Bible or the Talmud.

5:35   If a block quotation is introduced in text with quoted fragments interspersed with the words of the writer, the fragments must all have quotation marks at beginning and end. It is not permissible to begin a quotation in text with quotation marks at the beginning, as required, and to continue the quotation in block form, where ending punctuation marks are not used. Note the following example of *incorrect usage* in introducing the block quotation:

> Religion is just "the product of the craving to know whether these imaginary conceptions have realities answering to them in some other world than ours". And Mill continues, "Belief in a God or Gods
>> and in a life after death becomes the canvas which every mind . . . covers with such ideal pictures as it can either invent or copy.

The writer who is aware of this trap will take care that he does not introduce a quotation in text and complete it in block form. The way out may be as easy as it is here:

```
And Mill continues,
```

```
    Belief in a God or Gods and in a life after
    death becomes the canvas which every mind . . .
    covers with such ideal pictures as it can either
    invent or copy.
```

Sometimes the writer must rephrase his text or reconsider the amount to be quoted.

5:36   Two conditions under which a block quotation begins with paragraph indention are considered in paragraphs 5:33 and 5:34. When those conditions are not present, the first line of the block quotation is indented four spaces from the left marginal line, as shown in the example immediately above. Note that the first (partial) paragraph is the only one in a block quotation of more than one paragraph that may be set flush. All the others must be given paragraph indention, whether the quotation begins with the first sentence of the paragraph or at some point within it. If the latter, the paragraph opens with three ellipsis points begun after the four-space paragraph indention, as illustrated in paragraph 5:34.

5:37   If in a quotation of several paragraphs, there is an omission of a full paragraph or more, that omission should be indicated by a full stop and three ellipsis points at the end of the paragraph preceding the omission. Thus it may be possible that four dots at the end of a paragraph may be followed by three dots at the beginning of the next paragraph, as provided in paragraph 5:36 and illustrated in the last two paragraphs of the following example. This use of two consecutive sets of ellipsis points may occur in a block quotation, but not in a quotation that is run into text.

```
Recalling as an adult the time in his early youth
when a "new conscience" was forming. Merton writes:
```

```
        . . . A brand-new conscience was just coming
    into existence as an actual, operating function
    of a soul. My choices were just about to become
    responsible. . . .
        . . . since no man ever can, or could, live
```

> by himself and for himself alone, the destinies
> of thousands of other people were bound to be
> affected, some remotely, but some very directly
> and near-at-hand, by my own choices and decisions
> and desires, as my own life would also be formed
> and modified according to theirs.

5:38   If it is considered desirable to quote in block form fragments of prose which are widely scattered in the original source, a full line of ellipsis points may be used between the individual fragments.

INTERPOLATIONS

5:39   It is sometimes advisable for the writer to insert in a quotation a word or more of explanation, or clarification, or correction. All such insertions (interpolations) must be enclosed in square brackets. [ ]. Parentheses may *not* be substituted. Seeing a parenthetic element in a quotation, a reader assumes it was put there by the author of the source quoted. Words enclosed in square brackets indicate that the comment was put there by the person quoting the author. If your typewriter has no brackets, they must be inserted in the copy by hand, in permanent black ink.

5:40   To assure the reader that the faulty logic, error in fact, incorrect word, incorrect spelling, or the like, is in the original matter quoted, the Latin word *sic* ("so"; always underlined) may be placed in brackets after the error:

> "When the fog lifted, they were delighted to see
> that the country was heavily timbered and emmence
> [sic] numbers of fowl flying in every direction."

The use of *sic* should not be overdone. Quotations from sixteenth-century writing, for example, or from obviously archaic or illiterate writing, should not be strewn with *sic*s.

5:41   Interpolations made for purposes of clarification or correction are illustrated in the following:

> "But since these masters [Picasso, Braque, Matisse]
> appeared to be throwing away, rebelling against
> academic training, art teaching has itself been
> discredited."

"The recipient of the Nobel Peace Award for 1961
[1960] was Albert John Luthuli."

ITALICS (UNDERLINING)

5:42   Words that are not italicized in the original of the matter quoted may be italicized (underlined in typing) for emphasis desired by the writer of the paper. The source of the change should be indicated to the reader in one of three ways:
(1) By a notation enclosed in square brackets and placed immediately after the underlined words:

"This man described to me another large river
beyond the Rocky Mountains, the <u>southern branch</u>
[italics mine] of which he directed me to take."

(2) By a parenthetical note following the quotation:

"This man described to me another large river
beyond the Rocky Mountains, <u>the southern branch</u>
of which he directed me to take." (Italics mine.)

(3) By a footnote. Either a footnote or the scheme mentioned in (2) is preferable when italics have been added at two or more points in a quotation.

6   Footnotes

THE USE OF FOOTNOTES

6:1   Footnotes have four main uses: (*a*) to cite the authority for statements in text (specific facts or opinions as well as exact quotations); (*b*) to make cross-references; (*c*) to make incidental comments upon, to amplify or to qualify textual discussion—in short, to provide a place for material which the writer thinks it worthwhile to include but which he feels would disrupt the flow of thought if introduced into the text; (*d*) to make acknowledgements. Footnotes, then, are of two kinds: *reference* (*a* and *b* above), and *content* (*c* and *d* above). A content footnote may also include one or more references, as will be seen in the examples (para. 6:155). Interpretations and examples of footnote form are given in the following pages.

6:2   Unless it is short and uncomplicated, no table, outline, list, letter, or the like, should be placed in a footnote.

FOOTNOTE NUMBERS

6:3   The place in the text at which a footnote is introduced, whether of the reference or of the content category, should be marked with an arabic numeral. Place the numeral slightly above the line (but never a full space above), and do not put a period after it or embellish it with parentheses, brackets, or slashes. The numeral follows a punctuation mark, if any, except the dash, which it precedes.

6:4   The footnote number should follow the passage to which it refers. If the passage is an exact quotation, the footnote number comes at the end of the quotation, not after the author's name or at the end of the textual matter introducing the quotation.

6:5   Footnote numbers must follow one another in numerical order, beginning with figure one (1). Numbering may start on each page, or at the beginning of each chapter, or it may run continuously through the entire paper. There are possible complications in using the last two schemes, however, since if it was found that a note had been omitted, or that one should be deleted, it would be necessary to renumber the footnotes from the point of the desired change to the end of the chapter or of the paper. The insertion of a note numbered, for example, "1a" is not permissible, and the omission of a number likewise is not permissible.

POSITION OF FOOTNOTES

6:6   Footnotes should be arranged in numerical order at the foot of the page, and all those to which references are made in the text page must appear on the same page as the references to them.

An acceptable alternative is to convert the footnotes into endnotes by placing them at the end of the chapter or section to which they refer.

6:7   Reduction in the number of reference numbers in the text improves the appearance of the page and saves space in the footnote area as well as in typing time. Consider the spotty effect and the waste space resulting from a line or a column of *ibid.*'s. With careful planning, the number of footnotes and their bulk as well can often be considerably reduced without curtailing scholarly responsibilities. Three ways will be mentioned (paras. 6:8 – 10).

6:8   In a *single* paragraph containing several quotations from one work of the same author, a reference number following the last quotation would permit all the quotations to be cited in one footnote.

6:9   Instead of four reference numbers in the first example below, one number placed after the last name, as in the second example, would allow all four citations to be made in one footnote:

```
The means by which the traditional Western composers
have attempted to . . . communicate with their
audiences has been discussed at length . . . by
Eduard Hanslick,² Heinrich Schenker,³ Suzanne Langer,⁴
and Leonard Meyer,⁵ to name but a few.
```

```
The means by which the traditional Western composers
have attempted to . . . communicate with their
audiences has been discussed at length . . . by
Eduard Hanslick, Heinrich Schenker, Suzanne Langer,
and Leonard Meyer, to name but a few.²
```

The single footnote would then read:

```
     ²Eduard Hanslick, The Beautiful in Music, trans.
G. Cohen (New York: Novello, Ewer, 1891); Heinrich
Schenker, Der freie Satz, trans. and ed. T. H. Kreuger
(Ann Arbor: University Microfilms, 1960), pub. no.
60-1558; Suzanne Langer, Philosophy in a New Key
(New York: Mentor, 1959); Leonard B. Meyer, Emotion
and Meaning in Music (Chicago: University of Chicago
Press, 1956), and Music, the Arts, and Ideas (Chicago:
University of Chicago Press, 1967).
```

6:10   Tables, outlines, lists, letters, and the like that are not immediately relevant to the text are best placed in an appendix and referred to in the text by a simple footnote:

```
     ¹The member banks and their contributions are
listed in appendix 3.
```

6:11   If a block quotation (see para. 5:2) contains one or more footnote references from the original source, the corresponding footnotes should be placed beneath the quotation, not among the footnotes belonging to the paper itself. An eight-space rule should separate the footnote from the quotation, and the reference index, whether number or symbol, and the form of the footnote should follow exactly the style found in the original material:

```
They might all have said, along with Bataille himself:
```

```
          My tension, in a sense, resembles a great
     welling up of laughter, it is not unlike the
     burning passions of Sade's heroes, and yet, it
     is close to that of the martyrs, or of the
     saints.²³
          ²³"Ma tension ressemble, en un sens, à une
```

> folle envie de rire, elle diffère peu des
> passions dont brûlent les heros de Sade, et
> pourtant, elle est proche de celle des martyrs
> ou des saints." <u>Sur Nietzsche</u>, p. 12.

If the writer of the paper adds his own footnote references in a block quotation (to identify persons mentioned, for example, or to translate words or passages in a foreign language) the references are numbered in sequence with the other footnotes in the paper. The corresponding footnotes themselves are placed at the bottom of the page.

6:12   Specific directions for the typing of footnotes and for their correct placing on the page are given in the chapter on typing the paper (paras. 13:26–36).

REFERENCE FOOTNOTES

FIRST FULL REFERENCES

6:13   *Basic style.* The first time a work is mentioned in a footnote,[1] the entry should be in complete form; that is, it should include not only the author's full name, the title of the work, and the specific reference (i.e., volume, if any, and page number), but the facts of publication as well. Once a work has been cited in full, subsequent references to it should be in abbreviated form. These forms are fully discussed and illustrated in paragraphs 6:138–54.

6:14   With some exceptions, such as references to legal, classical, and biblical works, and to certain kinds of official publications, and references in scientific papers, all discussed hereafter, footnotes citing a published work the first time are given in the sequence indicated below. Although not every footnote entry will include all the items of information listed, the order should be maintained, regardless of the items omitted.

6:15   For a book, the source of the information, except the page number(s), should be the title page; for a periodical, it should be the cover and the article itself.

[1]Sample footnote references with corresponding bibliographical entries are shown in chapter 8.

6:16   *For a book*. The first, full reference to a book includes:
Name of author(s) (see paras. 6:19–29)[2]
Title of book (see paras. 6:30–34)
Name of editor, compiler, or translater, if any (see paras. 6:35–37)
Name of author of preface, introduction, or foreword, if any (see para. 6:38)
Name of series in which book appears, if any, with volume or number in the series (see paras. 6:39–40)
Number or name of edition, if other than the first (see paras. 6:43–48)
Total number of volumes, if more than one (see para. 6:49)
Facts of publication, consisting of
Place of publication (see paras. 6:51–55)
Name of publishing agency (see paras. 6:56–65)
Date of publication (see paras. 6:66–70)
Volume number, if any (see paras. 6:72–79)
Page number(s) of the specific citation (see paras. 6:81–84)

6:17   *For an article in a periodical.*[3] The first, full reference to an article in a periodical includes:
Name of author(s) (see paras. 6:19–29)
Title of article (see paras. 6:30–34)
Name of periodical (see paras. 6:30–32)
Volume number, if any (see paras. 6:32–33, 6:73–78)
Date of volume or issue (see paras. 6:32–33, 6:74–79)
Page number(s) (see paras. 6:74, 6:76, 6:81–86)

6:18   The items of information listed above for a book and for an article in a periodical are discussed in detail in the following paragraphs.

6:19   *Name of author(s).* Give the name(s) of the author(s) in normal order—Robert John Blank—and follow with a comma. Give the first name and initial of the second name (or first and second names), not initials only, except for well-known authors who habitually use only the initials of their

---

[2] The paragraph numbers in parentheses following each item refer to the detailed discussion.
[3] The discussion treats only of articles in journals and magazines. Newspapers are dealt with separately (paras. 6:97–100).

given names (e.g., T. S. Eliot, D. H. Lawrence, J. B. S. Haldane, W. B. Yeats). For an author whose first names appear on the title pages of some of his works, and initials only on others, footnote references to the latter should give the name as, for example, H[enry] R[obert] Anderson.

6:20   If the title page, or the heading of an article, gives a pseudonym known to be that of a certain author, the real name is used in the footnote and the pseudonym is enclosed in square brackets and placed after it (see example, para. 8:9). Such familiar pseudonyms as Anatole France, George Eliot, and Mark Twain should, however, be used in place of the real name.

6:21   If a pseudonym is indicated as such on the title page, the abbreviation "pseud." is enclosed in parentheses and placed after the name: Helen Delay (pseud.).

6:22   If pseudonymity is not indicated on the title page, but is nevertheless an established fact, the abbreviation "pseud." may be placed in brackets after the name: Helen Delay [pseud.].

6:23   If the title page gives no author's name, or if it designates the work as anonymous, and if in either case the authorship has been definitely established, the author's name, enclosed in square brackets, may be placed before the title: [Henry K. Black]. The use of "Anonymous" in place of the name of an author is not recommended. If the authorship is not reliably established, the footnote reference should begin with the title of the work.

6:24   For a work by two or by three authors, give the full names in normal order, separating the names of the two authors with "and"; of three authors, with commas, the last comma followed by "and":

Walter E. Houghton and G. Robert Stange

Bernard R. Berelson, Paul F. Lazarsfeld, and William N. McPhee

6:25   If a work has more than three authors, it is usual to cite in the footnote (but not in the bibliography), only the name of the author given first on the title page and to follow it with "et al." (*et alii*) or with the English equivalent, "and others". Note that the name of only the first-mentioned author should be given and that whether you choose to follow it with "et al." or with "and others", you should use the same style throughout the paper. No comma comes between the author's name and "et al.":

```
Gilbert W. King et al.     John Q. Smith and others
```

(See example, para. 8:6.)

6:26 For co-authors with the same surname, cite each name in full in the first reference—Sidney Webb and Beatrice Webb, not Sidney and Beatrice Webb. In later references, write Webb and Webb, not the Webbs.

6:27 Even though a title page may include after an author's name a title such as doctor, professor, president, or indicate a scholastic degree or an official position, all such designations should be omitted except in rare instances where one or more of them would have special significance for the subject of the paper.

6:28 The "author" may be a corporate body—a country, state, county, city, legislative body, institution, society, business firm, committee, or the like. (See example, para. 8:10.)

6:29 Some works, for example compilations and anthologies, are produced by compilers or editors, whose names appear in place of authors' names and are followed by the abbreviation "ed." (or "eds.") or "comp." (or "comps."):

```
Robert E. Kingery and Maurice F. Tauber, eds.
```

(See example, para. 8:11.)

6:30 *Title of the work.* Enter the full title of a book as it appears on the title page. Enter the title of an article as it appears at the head of the article, and follow with the name of the periodical, placing a comma between them. Adhere to the peculiarities, if any, of spelling and punctuation within the titles, but capitalize in accordance with the general rule as it applies to the titles of all classes of written works, whether they are published or in manuscript form (see paras. 4:5–12).

6:31   Underline the title of a whole published work, that is, the title of a book and the title of a periodical. Enclose in quotation marks the title of an article in a periodical. Place a comma after the title of a book unless it is followed immediately by parentheses enclosing the facts of publication, in which case the comma is placed after the final parenthesis:

> [1]Arthur C. Kirsch, Dryden's Heroic Drama (Princeton, N.J.: Princeton University Press, 1964), p. 15.

6:32   Place no comma between the title of a periodical and the volume number. If the volume number is further identified by a date, the date appears in parentheses.

6:33   A comma separates volume number from page number, and note that when the volume number is followed by a date enclosed in parentheses, the comma comes after the final parenthesis:

> [1]Samuel M. Thompson, "The Authority of Law", Ethics 75 (October 1964), 16-24.

> [2]William W. Crosskey, Politics and the Constitution in the History of the United States, 2 vols. (Chicago: University of Chicago Press, 1953), 1,48.

6:34   Since display headings, both on title pages and at the heads of articles, frequently set a title in two or more lines, and since punctuation is normally omitted at the ends of lines of display headings, it is often necessary to add marks of punctuation to a title as it will appear when written out in text or footnote or bibliography. This need occurs most often in titles composed of a main title and a subtitle. Consider the following example:

> The Early Growth of Logic in the Child
> Classification and Seriation

Here, as the title is shown on the title page, no punctuation follows *Child*. When it is copied without change from the title page, the title looks like this:

> Wrong: The Early Growth of Logic in the
> Child Classification and Seriation

Adding a colon after *Child* clarifies the meaning:

Right: The Early Growth of Logic in the
           Child: Classification and Seriation

6:35   *Name of editor, translator, or compiler.* If the title page contains in addition to the name of an author that of an editor, translator, or compiler, that name follows the title, being preceded by the appropriate abbreviation: "ed." or "trans." or "comp." In this case the abbreviation stands for "edited by" or "translated by" or "compiled by", and thus is never given in the plural form:

[1]Edward Chiera, They Wrote on Clay, ed.
George G. Cameron (Chicago: University of Chicago
Press, 1938), p. 42.

6:36   A work may have both an editor and a translator as well as an author, and the same person may be both editor and translator:

[1]Helmut Thielicke, Man in God's World, trans.
and ed. John W. Doberstein (New York and Evanston,
Ill.: Harper & Row, 1963), p. 43.

[2]August von Haxthausen, Studies on the Interior
of Russia, ed. S. Frederick Starr, trans. Eleanore
L. M. Schmidt (Chicago: University of Chicago Press,
1972), p. 47.

6:37   Similar in style is the entry of a work in which the author's name is included in the title. Here the author's name as the first item of information is omitted, although you might properly choose to insert it even though the title page omitted it:

[1]The Works of Shakespear, ed. Alexander Pope,
6 vols. (London: printed for Jacob Tonson in the
Strand, 1723-25), 2,38.

Or:

[1]Shakespeare, The Works of Shakespear, ed.
Alexander Pope, . . .

Although the foregoing arrangement, which gives the editor's name following the title of the work, is the form of reference most commonly used for this kind of work, it would be permissible in a paper dealing primarily with the work of Pope to give his name first, followed by "ed.":

¹Alexander Pope, ed., <u>The Works of Shakespear</u>, 6 vols. (London: printed for Jacob Tonson in the Strand, 1723-25), 2,38.

6:38   *Name of author of preface, foreword, or introduction.* If the title page of a book includes the name of the author of a preface, foreword, or introduction, that name is included in the reference. Note the style of the first of the following references, which is to Hammarskjöld's text:

¹Dag Hammarskjöld <u>Markings</u>, with a Foreword by W. H. Auden (New York: Alfred A. Knopf, 1964), p. 38.

The following reference, however, refers to the Foreword of the book, by W. H. Auden:

¹W. H. Auden, Foreword to <u>Markings</u>, by Dag Hammarskjöld (New York: Alfred A. Knopf, 1964), p. ix.

6:39   *Name of series.* Books and pamphlets are sometimes published as parts of named series (e.g., Oxford English Monographs, Yale Studies in Political Science, Monographs of the Society for Research in Child Development), which are sponsored by publishers, institutions (especially universities and graduate schools), governmental agencies, learned societies, commercial and industrial firms, and so on. Although a series bears some resemblance to a periodical publication and to a multivolume work as well, there are important differences stemming from their individual plans of publication—differences that are reflected in the particular style of reference appropriate to each. It may be helpful to describe briefly the three kinds of publications (paras. 6:40–42).

6:40   *Series.* The publication of a series is a continuing project of its sponsors, whose purpose is the issuing from time to time of books or pamphlets by different writers on topics which may range rather widely over a specific field, discipline or area of interest. Many series are numbered; the citation of a particular work in a numbered series should include the volume number (or issue number) after the name of the series. Note that the volume number here applies to the series and the page number to the book and therefore the citation differs from that for a multivolume work (see para 6:41). Note also that although the title of the work is underlined, the name of the series is neither underlined nor enclosed in quotation marks:

[1] Herbert Jacob, German Administration since Bismarck: Central Authority versus Local Autonomy, Yale Studies in Political Science, vol. 5 (New Haven, Conn.: Yale University Press, 1963), p. 124.

[2] National Industrial Conference Board, Research and Development, Studies in Business Economics, no. 82 (New York: National Industrial Conference Board, 1963), p. 21.

[3] Maximilian E. Novak, Defoe and the Nature of Man, Oxford English Monographs (London: Oxford University Press, 1963), p. 45.

6:41   *Multivolume work.* The publication of a multivolume work falls within limits that are more or less clearly defined in advance. The work consists, or will consist, of a number of volumes related to the same subject. All the volumes may be the work of one author and bear the same title (n.1); or they may be by one author and have different titles (n.2); or they may be by different authors and bear different titles, with the entire work carrying an overall title and having a general editor (n.3).

[1] Paul Tillich, Systematic Theology, 3 vols. (Chicago: University of Chicago Press, 1951-63), 2,48.

[2] Gerald E. Bentley, The Jacobean and Caroline Stage, vols. 1, 2: Dramatic Companies and Players; vols. 3-5: Plays and Playwrights; vol. 6: Theatres; vol. 7: Appendixes to Volume 6 and Indexes; 7 vols. (Oxford: Clarendon Press, 1941-68), 3,28.

[3] Gordon N. Ray, gen. ed., An Introduction to Literature, vol. 1: Reading the Short Story, by Herbert Barrows; vol. 2: The Nature of Drama, by Hubert Hefner; vol. 3: How Does a Poem Mean? by John Ciardi; vol. 4: The Character of Prose, by Wallace Douglas; 4 vols. (Boston: Houghton Mifflin Co., 1959), 2,47-48.

(See also para. 6:68.)

6:42 *Periodical.* A periodical is published at stated intervals (daily, weekly, monthly, quarterly, and so on), the issues being numbered in succession. In general, each issue of a magazine or journal is composed of articles by different authors. References to such articles follow the pattern set forth in paragraphs 6:31–33. The proper style for citing articles is not likely to raise any question except when an entire issue of a publication is devoted to one long paper, usually by one author. Sometimes such an issue replaces the more usual multi-article issue, bearing the number of that issue in the succession of numbers; sometimes it bears a supplementary number. In either case, its citation raises a question: Should the citation conform to the style used for a *whole* publication? The answer lies in the view taken by the publishers of the periodicals and by the libraries that a paper occupying a whole issue is published *in* the periodical. Thus it is cited as an article, except that the special designation shown on the cover of the particular issue is included in the reference (e.g., supplement, special issue, etc.):

[1]Elias Folker, "Report on Research in the Capital Markets", <u>Journal of Finance</u> 39, supplement (May 1964),15.

6:43 *Edition.* Information concerning the edition is required if the work cited is other than the first edition. The information is frequently printed on the title page, but it is often found on the copyright page (the reverse of the title page). Besides numbered editions, there are named editions, reprint editions, and paperback editions (paras. 6:44–48).

6:44 *Numbered editions.* Although new editions are usually numbered, they may be designated merely as New Edition, or New Revised Edition, and so on. Also found are: Second Edition, Revised; Revised Second Edition; Third Edition, Revised and Enlarged; Revised Edition in One Volume; Fourth Edition, Revised by John Doe; and so forth. The designations should be abbreviated in footnote and bibliographical entries: "new ed."; "new rev. ed."; "2nd ed., rev."; "rev. 2nd ed."; "3rd ed., rev. and enl."; "rev. ed. in 1 vol."; "4th ed., rev. John Doe"; and other variants:

¹Charles E. Merriam, New Aspects of Politics, 3rd ed., enl., with a Foreword by Barry D. Karl (Chicago: University of Chicago Press, 1972), p. 46.

²John Wight Duff, A Literary History of Rome from the Origins to the Close of the Golden Age, 3rd ed., edited by A. M. Duff (New York: Barnes and Noble, 1964), p. 86. [If "edited by" were not preceded by the edition number, the abbreviation "ed." would be used. See para. 6:35.]

6:45   *Reprint editions.* Works that are out of print are frequently reissued by publishers in special reprint editions. Footnote and bibliographical entries should note the reprint information and give also the date of the original publication and if possible the publisher:

¹Gunnar Myrdal, Population: A Problem for Democracy (Cambridge: Harvard University Press, 1940; reprint ed., Gloucester, Mass.: Peter Smith, 1956), p. 9.

It is not necessary to note a new printing—e.g., 4th impression—by the original publisher (see para. 6:66).

6:46   *Paperback editions.* Sometimes published at the same time as hardbound editions, sometimes at a later date, many paperback editions of scholarly works are now available. Since the paperback edition is sometimes a resetting or an abridgement of the hardbound work, the pagination of the two may differ. It is important, therefore, that any references to a paperback edition state that the work is a paperback and give the name of the edition, the publisher, and the date:

¹George F. Kennan, American Diplomacy, 1900-1950 (Chicago: University of Chicago Press, Phoenix Books, 1970), p. 48.

6:47   If a hardbound edition is used and the work is available in paperback, it may be helpful to your reader to include information on both editions:

¹George F. Kennan, American Diplomacy, 1900-1950 (Chicago: University of Chicago Press, 1951; also in paperback edition by the same publisher, Phoenix Books, 1970), pp. 80-82.

6:48   *Named editions.* Many classics are found in named editions. When they are used in references, they should be specified:

¹Blaise Pascal, <u>Pensées and The Provincial
Letters</u>, The Modern Library (New York: Random House,
1941), p. 418.

The title pages of some named editions do not give the name
of the publisher. If only city and date can be given, they are
separated by a comma.

6:49   *Number of volumes.* A reference to a multivolume work as a
whole should include the total number of volumes:

¹Paul Tillich, <u>Systematic Theology</u>, 3 vols.
(Chicago: University of Chicago Press, 1951–63).

A reference to one of the volumes may be in one of the two
styles discussed in paragraph 6:68.

6:50   *Facts of publication.* As listed in paragraph 6:16, the facts of
publication include the place (city), publisher, and date. They
appear in footnotes as follows:

(London: Hogarth Press, 1964)

These facts are given for printed books, monographs, and
pamphlets, and for published works that are mimeographed,
multigraphed, or otherwise produced by a copy-machine
process (see para. 4:16). But note the following exceptions:

Classical and biblical works	omit	all facts of publication
Legal works and some public documents	usually omit	all but the date
Dictionaries, general encyclopaedias, and atlases	omit	all but edition and date
In certain disciplines and in certain fields, the citations	omit	name of publisher
Periodicals, in general	omit	all but the date

6:51   *Place of publication.* If the names of two or more cities
appear under the publisher's imprint, the first-named is the

location of the editorial offices, and that is normally all that need be given in the reference. But all the names mentioned may be included, as, for example, "Oxford, London, and New York." Do not assume, however, that London and New York may properly be added when Oxford alone appears on the title page.

6:52 With American publications, if the city is not generally well known, give the state as well, using the standard abbreviation for the state, as "Glencoe, Ill." "Cambridge" would imply "Cambridge, England". Identify the American Cambridge by writing "Cambridge, Mass." unless it is followed by "Harvard University Press" or "M.I.T. Press".

6:53 For foreign cities, use the English name if there is one: Cologne, not Köln; Munich, not München; Florence, not Firenze; Padua, not Padova; Milan, not Milano; Rome, not Roma; Vienna, not Wien; Prague, not Praha; and so forth.

6:54 If neither the title page nor the copyright page gives the place of publication, write "n.p." (for "no place") as the first item of information on facts of publication. Follow it with a colon if a publisher is given, with a comma if only the date follows.

6:55 The abbreviation "n.p." may also stand for "no publisher". If both place and publisher are missing, "n.p." with the date tells the whole story.

6:56 *Name of publishing agency.*[4] The name of the publisher may be given either in the style used by the company itself or in the accepted abbreviated form as it is given for British publishers in the annual volume of *British National Bibliography* and in *British Books in Print,* and for American publishers in *Books in Print*, issued annually by R. R. Bowker Co.

6:57 Note carefully the spelling and punctuation of publishers' names. There is no comma in Houghton Mifflin Co., for example; but there is a comma in the name of Little, Brown &

---

[4]The broader term, "publishing agency", rather than "publisher", is used here because some of the works are published by societies, institutions of learning, commerce, banking, and the like, which are not publishers per se. The terms are used interchangeably in the text of the section.

Co., and in that of Harcourt, Brace & Co., as the firm was formerly known. Hyphens separate the names in McGraw-Hill Book Co. and in Appleton-Century-Crofts. There is a small "m", not a capital "M", in the middle of Macmillan.

6:58 Even though you may choose to write publishers' names in full, it is customary to omit an initial "The" and the abbreviation "Inc." or "Ltd" or "S.A."; to use the ampersand (&) in place of "and"; and to abbreviate "Company" to "Co." and "Brother" or "Brothers" to "Bro." or "Bros". Whatever the style chosen, it must be used consistently throughout the paper.

6:59 If the title page indicates that a work was co-published, the reference should give both publishers:

(New York: Alfred A. Knopf and Viking Press, 1966)

(Boston: Ginn & Co., 1964; Montreal: Round Press, 1964)

6:60 The title page of a book issued by a subsidiary of a publisher gives both names, and references to such a book should include both:

(Cambridge: Harvard University Press, Belknap Press, 1965)

6:61 If a work was published for an institution, society, or the like, and their name appears on the title page together with the publisher's name, the references should include both names:

(New York: Columbia University Press for the American Geographical Society, 1947)

6:62 If a work has been reprinted at a date later than that of its original publication, the fact will usually be noted on the entry card for the work in the catalogue at your library. Such information is especially useful for locating some hard-to-find old works. (See para. 6:45 for the style of reference used in citing a reprint edition.)

6:63 Do not substitute the present name of a publishing firm for that shown on the title page of the work being cited.

6:64 Do not translate parts of the names of foreign publishers, even when you have anglicized the name of the city (para.

6:53). Do not, for example, change "Compagnie" or "Cie", to "Company" or "Co."; or "et Frère" to "and Brother" or "and Bro."

6:65 Certain disciplines and certain fields, in accord with long-established practice, commonly omit names of publishers from their references. Thus, only place and date of publication appear, as, for example, "New York, 1970". Note that when only two facts of publication are given, they are separated with a comma.

6:66 *Date of publication.* The date usually appears on the title page, either with the publisher's imprint or overleaf in the copyright data. There may be more than one copyright date; if so, the last is the one under which the work in hand was issued. But there may also be one or more dates shown in addition to the date of copyright. Since those refer to *reprintings,* or new impressions, not new editions, they should be disregarded. The date of copyright is the one to use in your reference—unless a different date appears with the publisher's imprint on the title page; the latter would then be the one to use. If no date is shown anywhere, write "n.d." (for "no date"):

(New York: Grosset & Dunlap, n.d.)

6:67 If, however, the date has been established by means other than the title page or copyright page, place the date in square brackets. The entry for the work in the catalogue at your library often carries the date of publication when the title page omits it. When the date has been discovered through the efforts of the library, it will be shown on the entry card in square brackets. In a footnote it is given thus:

(New York: Grosset & Dunlap, [1931])

6:68 It has been noted that a first reference to a multivolume work includes the total number of volumes (para. 6:49) together with the facts of publication. If the individual volumes have been issued in different years, reference to a volume number must indicate that fact by a footnote in the following form:

[1]Paul Tillich, <u>Systematic Theology</u>, 3 vols. (Chicago: University of Chicago Press, 1951-63), 2 (1957), 182.

6:69   Since all the volumes of the multivolume work mentioned in the following note were published in one year, there is no need to repeat the publication date of the volume cited:

> ³Gordon N. Ray, gen. ed., <u>An Introduction to Literature</u>, 4 vols. (Boston: Houghton Mifflin Co., 1959), vol. 2: <u>The Nature of Drama</u>, by Hubert Hefner, pp. 47–49.

(Here "vol." and "pp." are used because they do not refer to the same title: "vol. 2" means the second volume of *An Introduction to Literature* and "pp. 47–49" refers to that volume itself, *The Nature of Drama*.)

6:70   When the publication of a multivolume work is not complete, give the date when publication began and follow with a dash: 1968–

6:71   References to periodicals normally omit place and publisher (newspaper names may, however, include place; see para. 6:97), except that for foreign periodicals of limited circulation, and titles that are identical or similar to periodicals published elsewhere, the place of publication should be included:

> ¹Jack Fishman, "Un grand homme dans son intimité: Churchill", <u>Historia</u> (Paris), no. 220 (November 1964), pp. 684–94.

6:72   *Volume number.* Reference to a work of more than one volume must give the volume number as well as the page(s). If the reference is the first to the work, include the facts of publication.

6:73   As shown in examples on previous pages, volume numbers are expressed in arabic numerals rather than roman. In scientific, technical, and legal writing, the more convenient arabic numerals replaced the roman some years ago, and gradually in other fields as well the arabic numerals have been adopted. Volume numbers of books and periodicals, then, should be given in arabic numerals, regardless of whether they are expressed in roman or in arabic in the works cited.

6:74   Omit the abbreviations "vol." and "p." or "pp." when a reference cites both volume and page(s) of the same work. Now, if both are shown in arabic numerals and no identifying abbreviations are used, some way of distinguishing volume from page is clearly necessary. Give volume number first and page number second and separate them with a comma:

> [1]Don Swanson, "Dialogue with a Catalogue",
> Library Quarterly 34 (December 1963),113-25.

When the volume number is followed directly by a parenthesis, as it is in this example, the comma comes after the parenthesis rather than before. (See also para. 6:68).

6:75   References to magazines and journals that are issued weekly, monthly, bimonthly, quarterly, and so on, should give the volume number in arabic numerals immediately after the title of the publication (see example in para. 6:74). Ordinarily, the date (month and year) is enclosed in parentheses and placed immediately after the volume number. Note that there is no mark of punctuation between the title of the publication and the volume number, and none between month and year.

6:76   The number of the issue need not be given, unless the periodical is one that is numbered *only by issue,* not by volume and issue. The reference to such a periodical should give the issue number followed by the year date in parentheses:

> [1]Konrad Lorenz, "The Wisdom of Darwin",
> Midway, no. 22 (1965), p. 48.

Note that when issue number rather than volume is given, a comma separates it from the title of the periodical; also that page number is preceded by the abbreviation "p." or "pp."

6:77   Some periodicals publish volumes in successive series, each beginning with volume 1. In some cases the successive series are numbered; in some they are lettered; and in some they are designated as "Old Series" or "New Series", abbreviated as "o.s." and "n.s.":

94

[1]J. Durbin, "Estimation of Parameters in
Time Series Regression Models", Journal of the
Royal Statistical Society, ser. B. 22 (January
1960),139-53.

6:78 Magazines of general interest, even though they may carry
volume numbers, are best identified by date alone. The date
then takes the place of the volume number and is not enclosed
in parentheses:

[1]Barbara W. Tuchman, "If Asia Were Clay in
the Hands of the West", Atlantic, September 1970,
pp. 68-84.

6:79 Daily newspapers and weekly magazines are also identified by
date alone:

[1]Palo Alto (Calif.) Times, 19 November, 1970.

Note also paragraphs 6:97–100 "Newspapers".

[2]Franklin D. Murphy, "Yardsticks for a New
Era", Saturday Review, 21 November 1970, pp. 23-25.

6:80 *Forthcoming work.* If a writer finds it desirable to mention a
work that has been accepted for publication but is not yet
published, he may do so in the following style for a book:

[1]Marshall Hodgson, The Venture of Islam
(Chicago: University of Chicago Press, forthcoming).

And for a journal article:

[2]Robert D. Hume, "Theory of Comedy in the
Restoration", Modern Philology, forthcoming.

6:81 *Page number(s).* Refer to a single page as, for example,
"p. 60". Refer to inclusive page numbers in accordance with
the scheme set forth in paragraph 2:52.

6:82 Use exact inclusive page numbers in preference to such
designations as "pp. 80f." (p. 80 and following page) or "pp.
82, 83ff." (pp. 82, 83, and following pages). Since "f." refers
to only a single page immediately following the number given,

the exact pages should be cited: "pp. 80–81". Similarly, avoid using "pp. 82, 83 ff.", by giving inclusive pages, "pp. 82–85", for example.

6:83 In cases where an article begins in the front of a magazine and then continues at the back, after other (unrelated) material, pagination should be shown in this form: "pp. 36–45, 56".

6:84 The word "passim" ("here and there") should be used with discretion. Employ it only in referring to information scattered over a considerable stretch of text, or throughout a chapter or other long section. Give the inclusive page numbers or the chapter number and place "passim" at the end of the reference:

```
Haxthausen, Studies on the Interior of Russia,
chap. 9 passim.

Kennan, American Diplomacy, pp. 80-85 passim, 92,
105.
```

Note that passim is a whole word, not an abbreviation, and that it is not underlined.

6:85 *Omission of abbreviations "vol." and "p."* In a reference that includes both a volume and a page number, the abbreviations "vol." and "p." or "pp." are usually omitted (see para. 6:74). In some kinds of references, however, these abbreviations are needed. For example, in the following reference, the volume number is that of the series, not that of the particular work. The abbreviations should be used:

```
¹Leonard L. Watkins, Commercial Banking Reform
in the United States, Michigan Business Studies,
vol. 8, no. 5 (Ann Arbor: University of Michigan,
1938), p. 464.
```

And in the following reference, the citation of the title and facts of publication of the particular volume requires the fuller treatment:

```
¹Gabriel Marcel, The Mystery of Being, vol. 2:
Faith and Reality (Chicago: Henry Regnery Co., 1960),
pp. 19-20.
```

(See also the example in para. 6:69).

6:86   When in addition to volume and page another division of a work is necessary to determine the page reference, that division must be appropriately designated even though the abbreviations "vol." and "p." are omitted:

> [1]Donald Lach, <u>Asia in the Making of Europe</u> (Chicago: University of Chicago Press, 1965–), 2. bk.1, 165.

6:87   *Numerals used for other parts of works.* The use of arabic rather than roman numerals to indicate volume numbers is noted in paragraph 6:73. It is not volume numbers only that are now shown in arabic numerals, but (with some few exceptions) all the divisions of a written work: parts, volumes, books, chapters, pages; acts and scenes of a play; lines and stanzas of a poem; columns of a tabulation; plates, figures, tables, maps; and so on. There are three exceptions: (1) Reference to a book's preliminary pages which are numbered with small roman numerals should use the same style of numeral. (2) References to divisions of official documents or manuscript materials should follow the numbering style of the source. (3) Citation of a collection of inscriptions, papyri, or ostraca that is divided into volumes should use roman numerals for the volume numbers (para. 6:113).

SPLIT REFERENCES

6:88   If at the first reference to a work the author's full name is brought into the text close to the footnote number, it may be omitted from the note. Later in the text, the appearance of only the author's surname permits its omission from the footnote. And similarly, if both the name of the author and the title of the work are given in the text, they may be omitted from the footnote, which then would consist of the facts of publication (if it is the first reference to the work) plus the page number(s), or volume and page(s), if appropriate.

ABBREVIATIONS IN FOOTNOTES, BIBLIOGRAPHIES, AND SO ON

USE OF ABBREVIATIONS

6:89   It was pointed out earlier (para. 2:1) that except in scientific and technical writing, few abbreviations are permissible in text, but that in footnote and bibliographical entries, in tabular matter, and in some kinds of illustrative matter, abbreviations are normally preferred to complete words. Listed below are some abbreviations commonly found in these places. In using them, note the following:

6:90   An abbreviation designating a part of a written work (vol., pt, chap., etc.) should never be used unless it is followed or preceded by a number (vol. 2, pt 1, chap. 10, pp. 9–11, 4 vols., etc.). When used without numbers these words should be spelled out.

6:91   Of the abbreviations in the following list only "MS" is capitalized at all times, but each abbreviation should begin with a capital when it is the first word of a footnote and whenever the usual rules for capitalization apply.

6:92   The word *sic* is underlined, but not the Latin abbreviations commonly used in footnotes, bibliographies, tabular matter, and so on.

LIST OF ABBREVIATIONS

6:93   app., appendix
art., article (plural, arts.)
b., born
bk, book (plural, bks)
c., copyright: <u>chapter</u>, in legal documents only:
    <u>circa</u>, about, approximately
cf., <u>confer</u>, compare (Note that <u>confer</u> is the Latin
    word for "compare"; cf. must not be used as the
    abbreviation for the English "confer", nor
    should cf. be used to mean "see")(para.6: 157)
ch., chapter, (plural, chs.)
col., column (plural, cols.)
comp., compiler (plural, comps.); compiled by

dept, department (plural, depts)
d., died
div., division (plural, divs.)
e.g., exempli gratia, for example
ed., edition; edited by; editor (plural, eds.)
et al., et alii, and others
et seq., et sequens, and the following
etc., et cetera, and so forth
fig., figure (plural, figs.)
ibid., ibidem, in the same place (para. 6:138-142, 158)
id., idem, the same (used to refer to persons,
     except in law citations; not to be confused
     with ibid.) (para. 6:140-141)
i.e., id est, that is
infra, below
l.(ell), line (plural, ll.) (Not recommended because
     the abbreviation might be mistaken for "one"
     and the plural for "eleven.")
loc. cit., loco citato, in the place cited (para. 6:138)
MS, manuscript (plural, MSS)
n., note, footnote (plural, nn.)
n.d., no date
n.p., no place; no publisher
no., number (plural, nos.)
n.s., new series
op. cit., opere citato, in the work cited (para. 6:138)
o.s., old series
p., page (plural·, pp.)
para., paragraph (plural, paras.)
passim, here and there
pt, part (plural, pts)
q.v., quod vide, which see
sc., scene
sec., section (plural, secs.)
sic, so, thus
supp., supplement (plural, supps.)
supra, above
s.v., sub verbo, sub voce, under the word
trans., translator; translated by
v., verse (plural, vv.), also versus, against
viz., videlicet, namely
vol., volume (plural, vols.)
vs, versus, against (v. in law references)

ABBREVIATIONS OF TITLES

6:94   Titles of journals, dictionaries, and other sources used
frequently in a paper may be abbreviated by the initials of the

words of their names, without spaces or periods between the letters. Such abbreviations are permissible in footnotes but not in bibliographical entries:

```
AHR, American Historical Review
NRF, Nouvelle Revue Française
DNB, Dictionary of National Biography
OED, Oxford English Dictionary
```

Journals that have initials as actual titles should be so cited in both footnotes and bibliographies.

```
PMLA     MLN     ELH
```

6:95   Also, it is permissible for a writer who must refer frequently to the same work to devise an abbreviation to be used after the first full reference:

```
Christopher Addison, Four and a Half Years, 2 vols.
(London: Hutchinson & Co., 1934), 1,35 (hereafter
cited as Addison, Diary).
```

See also para. 6:154.

CITATION TAKEN FROM A SECONDARY SOURCE

6:96   In citing the work of one author as found in that of another, both the work in which the reference was found (secondary source) and the title of the work mentioned therein must be given in the reference. In general, the style illustrated in footnote 1 should be followed, but if it is more significant for the purposes of the paper to emphasize Hulbert's citing of the *Jesuit Relations*, the style of the second footnote should be used:

```
  1
   Jesuit Relations and Allied Documents,
vol. 59, n. 41, quoted in [or "cited by"] Archer
Butler Hulbert, Portage Paths (Cleveland: Arthur
H. Clark, 1903), p. 181.
  2
   Archer Butler Hulbert, Portage Paths
(Cleveland: Arthur H. Clark, 1903), p. 181,
quoting [or "citing"] Jesuit Relations and
Allied Documents, vol. 59, n. 41.
```

SPECIAL FORMS

NEWSPAPERS

6:97   For reference to a newspaper, the name of the paper and the date are usually sufficient; but many large metropolitan papers, especially Sunday editions, are made up in sections that are separately paginated. For these, section number (or letter) and page number must be given. It is convenient for the reader if the title of the article and the author, if any, are included in the reference:

"Amazing Amazon Region", <u>New York Times</u>, 12 January 1969, sec. 4. p. E11.

If the name of the newspaper does not include the name of the city, place it before the newspaper title and underline title only:

Torquay <u>Herald Express</u>   Bolton <u>Evening News</u>

If the city is not well known, give the name of the county or state in parentheses:

<u>Menlo Park</u> (Calif.) <u>Recorder</u>

<u>Golspie</u> (Sutherland) <u>Northern Times</u>

If the name of the city is the same as that of another well-known city, give after it the name of the county, state and/or country in parentheses:

<u>Richmond</u> (Surrey, UK) <u>Herald</u>
<u>Richmond</u> (Virginia, USA) <u>News Leader</u>

6:98   For foreign newspapers in which the city of publication does not form a part of the title, the name of the city should be given in parentheses after the title:

<u>Le Monde</u> (Paris)   but: <u>Frankfurter Zeitung</u>
<u>La Stampa</u> (Milan)

6:99   The city of publication need not be given for such well-known newspapers as the *Times*, the *Observer*, the *Christian Science Monitor*, and the *Wall Street Journal*.

Outside the United Kingdom the two English newspapers would be given as *Times* (London) and *Observer* (London).

6:100   An initial "The" in English language newspaper titles is omitted, but its equivalent in a foreign language is retained:

thus, *Times* (London), but *Le Monde* (Paris). This practice holds for footnote and bibliographical entries, but when a newspaper (or journal or magazine) title appears in the text, "the" may precede if the syntax requires it, but it is not treated as part of the title:

The Sunday Telegraph gives superior coverage to foreign news.

He prefers New York Times editorials to those of any other newspaper.

ARTICLES IN ENCYCLOPAEDIAS AND DICTIONARIES

6:101   In citing alphabetically arranged reference works such as encyclopaedias and dictionaries, it is best to give the title of the article preceded by "s.v." (*sub verbo*, "under the word") rather than volume and page numbers. Place of publication, publisher's name, and in certain cases the date, are omitted from citations of most reference works. The edition, unless it is the first, is normally mentioned. But here a word is in order concerning the policy of "continuous revision" under which the major encyclopaedias have operated for some years. The number of the edition is not mentioned on their title pages, and the date of publication thus becomes the means of identification. When the title page gives the number of the edition, the reference should include it (n. 1 below); when it does not mention the edition, identify the particular work by date of publication (n. 2). In referring to a signed article, the name of the author may be included. If only the author's initials appear beneath the article, the list of authors in the front matter of the work may provide the name:

[1] Encyclopaedia Britannica, 11th ed., s.v. "Blake, William", by J. W. Comyns-Carr.

[2] Encyclopedia Americana, 1963 ed., s.v. "Sitting Bull".

[3] Columbia Encyclopedia, 3rd ed., s.v. "Cano, Juan Sebastian del".

[4] Webster's Geographical Dictionary, rev. ed. (1964), s.v. "Dominican Republic".

NOVELS

6:102   Novels are best referred to by chapter (or by part or book as well as chapter), since many appear in various editions differently paginated:

> [1]Joseph Conrad, <u>Heart of Darkness</u> (New York: Doubleday, Page & Co., 1903), chap. 3.

References to modern novels may cite page numbers, but be sure to include the facts of publication (see paras. 6:50–71).

> [2]John Cheever, <u>Bullett Park</u> (New York: Alfred A. Knopf, 1969), p. 139.

PLAYS AND LONG POEMS

6:103   References to modern plays follow the style used for books, except that act, scene, and line numbers are given instead of pages:

> [1]Louis O. Coxe and Robert Chapman, <u>Billy Budd</u> (Princeton: Princeton University Press, 1951), act 1, sc. 2, line 83.

6:104   For English classics, both plays and long poems, the style of reference may be that used for Greek and Latin classical works (see paras. 6:106–14). If the work is recognized as that of a widely known author, the author's name is frequently omitted; the title is underlined, whether the work is published as a separate volume or as part of a collection, and the facts of publication are seldom given. Among the works so treated are the plays of Shakespeare and of Jonson and such long poems as *The Faerie Queene, Paradise Lost, The Ring and the Book*:

> <u>Romeo and Juliet</u> 3. 2. 1–30
>   or:
> <u>Romeo and Juliet</u>, act 3, sc. 2, lines 1–30
>
> <u>Paradise Lost</u> 1. 83–86
>   or:
> <u>Paradise Lost</u>, bk 1, lines 83–86

SHORT POEMS

6:105   Short poems, which most often are published in collections, show the title placed between quotation marks and the name of the collection underlined. Stanza and lines are designated:

```
Francis Thompson, "The Hound of Heaven", in The
Oxford Book of Modern Verse (Oxford: Clarendon Press,
1936), stanza 3, lines 11-21.
```

GREEK AND LATIN CLASSICAL WORKS

6:106   References to classical works use abbreviations extensively for: author's name; title of the work; collections of inscriptions, papyri, ostraca, and so on; and for the titles of well-known periodical publications and other reference tools. For a list of accepted abbreviations, the *Oxford Classical Dictionary* should be consulted. It is recommended, however, that such abbreviations should not be used except in papers on predominantly classical topics. Sample footnotes appear in paragraph 6:114 below.

6:107   Titles of individual works, collections, and periodicals are underlined, whether they are given in full or abbreviated. In Greek and Latin titles, only the first word, proper nouns, and proper adjectives are capitalized.

6:108   The different levels of division of a work (book, part, section, chapter, lines, etc.) are indicated with *arabic* numerals. When designated by number only, the different levels are separated with periods:

```
Stat. Silv. 1. 3. 32
```

In a succession of references to the same level, commas separate with several references:

```
Ovid Met. 1. 240, 242
```

A hyphen separates continuing numbers (see para. 6:114, n. 1). If for the sake of clarity, identifying abbreviations are used before the numbers, the several divisions are separated with commas, not periods (bk. 2, sec. 4).

6:109   There is no punctuation between the author's name and the title of the work, and none between the title of the work and the first reference unless the reference is preceded by an identifying abbreviation, in which case a comma intervenes.

6:110   In general, the facts of publication are omitted, but the name of the edition may be given after the title (para. 6:114, n. 4), and it *must be given* if the reference is made to page numbers rather than to book, chapter, and so on.

6:111   The number of an edition, other than the first, is indicated by a superior number placed either after the title or after the volume number if the reference includes volume number (para. 6:114, nn. 7, 8).

6:112   A superior letter or figure placed immediately after a number referring to a division of a work indicates a subdivision (para. 6:114, n. 9). If preferred, the letters may be placed on the line, and either capital or small letters may be used, the choice depending upon usage in the source cited.

6:113   Despite the preference indicated in this *Manual* for arabic numerals rather than roman for volume numbers (see para. 6:87), references to collections of inscriptions, papyri, ostraca, and so forth, should continue to express volume numbers in capital roman numerals. After the volume number comes the document number, followed by numbers indicating the remaining divisions to which reference is made. Note that a comma separates title from volume number, and a comma also separates volume number from document number, after which full stops separate the remaining divisions (see para. 6:114, n. 6).

6:114   The following examples illustrate points discussed in paragraphs 6:106–13:

[1]Homer <u>Odyssey</u> 9. 266-71.

   <u>or</u>:

[2]Hom. <u>Od</u>. 9. 266-71.

[3]Cicero <u>De officiis</u> 2. 133, 140.

[4]Horace <u>Satires, Epistles and Ars poetica</u>,
Loeb Classical Library, p. 12.

[5]H. Musurillo TAPA 93 (1926): 231.

[6]IG Rom., III, 739. 9. 10, 17. [This refers
to Inscriptiones Graecae ad res Romanas pertinentes,
vol. III, document 739, section 9, lines 10 and 17.]

[7]E. Meyer Kleine Schriften 1[2] (Halle, 1924),
382.

[8]Stolz-Schmalz Lat. Gram.[5] (rev. Leumann-
Hofmann; Munich, 1928), pp. 490-91.

[9]Aristotle Poetics 20. 1456[b]20. 34-35.

[10]POxy. 1485. [POxy. = Oxyrhynchus Papyri.
The number cited is that of the document number;
there is no volume number.]

MEDIEVAL WORKS

6:115   References to medieval works may be in the same style as that
used for Greek and Latin classical works:

[1]Irenaeus Against Heresies 1. 8. 3.

[2]John of the Cross Ascent of Mount Carmel
(trans. E. Allison Peers) 2. 20. 5.

[3]Beowulf, lines 2401-7. [When the specific
part is named, a comma separates title from
reference.]

SCRIPTURAL REFERENCES

6:116   Exact references to the Bible and the Apocrypha use
abbreviations for the books both in text and in footnotes.
Chapter and verse, separated with a colon, are both indicated
with arabic numerals. The King James version is assumed
unless another is mentioned. There is no underlining:

[1]Psalm 103:6-14.

[2]1 Cor. 13:1-13 (NEB). [NEB = New English
Bible.]

Non-Christian sacred scriptures are referred to in the same
manner as Christian.

RADIO AND TELEVISION PROGRAMMES

6:117   The title of a radio or television programme is quoted, following the name of the station or of the broadcasting network given in abbreviation. If a specific programme is referred to, the date is included; and if it is particularly significant for the textual discussion, more information may be given:

> [1]Granada TV, "Coronation Street".
>
> [2]BBC-TV, "Panorama", 7 January 1980.
>
> [3]CBS, "Twentieth Century", 28 October 1962, "I Remember: Dag Hammarskjöld", Walter Cronkite.

MICROFORM REPRODUCTIONS

6:118   Much valuable written material, both of historical and of temporary interest, is preserved in microform. A considerable amount of this material has seen earlier publication in the form of a book or a magazine or a newspaper that could be held in the hand; much also is published only in microform. References to micropublications that are republications of earlier published material should give the relevant facts of the original publication, if available, plus the facts concerning the micropublisher and the publication order number. The titles should be underlined or enclosed in quotation marks as may be suitable for the type of work cited (see paras. 4:16–29). References to works published only in microform should give the facts of publication for the micropublisher and the publication order number. Titles should be underlined:

> [1]Godwin C. Chu and Wilbur Schramm, Learning from Television: What the Research Says (Bethesda, Md.: ERIC Document Reproduction Service, ED 014 900, 1967).
>
> [2]Paul Tillich, ·The Interpretation of History (New York: Charles Scribner's Sons, 1936; Ann Arbor, Mich.: University Microfilms, OP 2783, n.d.).

MANUSCRIPT COLLECTIONS

6:119   References to manuscript collections give as a minimum the name of the city in which the depository is located, the name of the depository, and the name or number (or both) of the collection. When a specific document is cited, it is best to mention it first and to include the pertinent facts. If the document has a title, it is in quotation marks; if there is a general designation, such as *diary, letter, telegram, memorandum*, the word is capitalized but not in quotation marks or underlined. Note the difference between the order of the items in a footnote that mentions a specific document and one that does not. (The same collection is used for both examples.)

[1]Gen. Joseph C. Castner, "Report to the War Department, 17 January 1927", Modern Military Records Division, Record Group 94, National Archives, Washington, D.C.

[2]Washington, D.C., National Archives, Modern Military Records Division, Record Group 94.

[3]Stanley K. Hornbeck, Memorandum on Clarence Gauss, 8 May 1942, Hornbeck Papers, File "Gauss", Hoover Library, Stanford, California.

Do not use the word "letter" if the reference gives names of sender and recipient and date of communication:

[4]Frank Vanderlip to Robert Lansing, 2 September 1915, Frank Vanderlip Papers, Columbia University Library, New York.

MISCELLANEOUS UNPUBLISHED MATERIALS

6:120   Because of their variety, manuscript materials are cited in different forms. If the material has a title, that title is placed within quotation marks, following the name of the sponsoring organization or of the author, if any. If there is a descriptive title, it is not in quotation marks. Mention of the nature of the material follows the title, and although exact location (such as page numbers) can seldom be given, the citation should, if possible, include information which would permit the material to be found. The information given about a personal letter may be much or little, depending upon its value as source material (see nn. 1 and 2).

[1] John Blank, personal letter.

[2] Alan Cranston, California State Controller, to Maurice Sexton, Sacramento, 22 October 1962, Personal Files of Maurice Sexton, Modesto, California.

[3] Morristown (Kansas) Orphans' Home, Minutes of Meetings of the Board of Managers, Meeting of 6 May 1930.

[4] Sidney E. Mead, "Some Eternal Greatness", sermon preached at the Rockefeller Chapel, University of Chicago, 31 July 1960.

[5] O. C. Phillips, Jr., "The Influence of Ovid on Lucan's Bellum civile" (Ph.D. dissertation, University of Chicago, 1962), p. 14.

INTERVIEWS

6:121   References to interviews include the name of the person or the group interviewed, the place, and the date.

[1] A. A. Wyler, interview held during meeting of the American Astronomical Society, Pasadena, California, June 1964.

[2] Farmers' State Bank, Barrett, Nebraska, interviews with a selected list of depositors, August 1960.

LEGAL CITATIONS

6:122   Law publications use a style of citation very different from that of other fields. Space permits no more than a brief treatment of legal citations here, and the materials chosen for illustration are, therefore, those which it is thought may be most useful to the student. For United Kingdom and Commonwealth law the most authoritative guide to citation practice is the *Manual of Legal Citations* (London, 1959–60) published by the University of London Institute of Advanced Legal Studies.

For American practice the student should consult the current edition of the guide published by the Harvard Law Review Association: *A Uniform System of Citation.*

The style of reference set out here follows the Institute of Advanced Legal Studies' *Manual* in most respects: where it differs, the changes are due largely to the fact that here guidance is being offered to students using a typewriter rather than to those preparing copy for printing.

6:123   A conspicuous feature of legal reference usage is that of abbreviations for the titles of law reports, periodicals and leading treatises, and for the names of courts and legislative bodies. *The Manual of Law Librarianship: the Use and Organization of Legal Literature*, edited by Elizabeth M. Moys and published for the British and Irish Association of Law Libraries (London: André Deutsch, 1976), contains a list of the most used and most reliable sources of such abbreviations. Sweet and Maxwell's *Guide to Law Reports and Statutes* (London: Sweet and Maxwell Ltd, 4th ed., 1962) is the source most generally used by legal practitioners, although the Institute of Advanced Legal Studies' *Manual* has a more complete list.

6:124   The styles of reference given in the examples in this section are those appropriate for footnotes. In the text, and in textual matter for footnotes, titles of all publications of whatever kind (books, periodicals, reports, documents) are underlined. Items such as periodical titles, which are abbreviated in footnotes, are spelled out in all textual matter. However, although the names of parties to court cases are underlined in textual matter, the linking "v." is never underlined, although in a Table of Cases it would be underlined. Law reports are always identified by their abbreviations, whether in textual matter or in footnotes, and these abbreviations are never underlined.

6:125   Papers on topics that are predominantly legal should employ the style of reference discussed in this section, but when papers in other fields refer to books and periodicals in the field of law, as is frequently done in the social sciences for example, the references to legal works should be adapted to that of the topic field in order to preserve a uniform style. References to legal sources, legislation and law reports should, however, always follow legal conventions.

6:126 A paper in the field of law may have occasion to refer to official publications other than those mentioned above. In such cases, the discussion and examples in chapter 9 may be useful. The forms of citation listed there would require change to legal style, as set forth in this section.

6:127 *Legislation.* Acts of Parliament are cited somewhat differently according to their type and their date of enactment. All modern Public General Acts should be cited by their official short titles, which are given in the short title sections found at the end of statutes, and usually also given at the heads of statutes. Most of the surviving older statutes have been assigned short titles by the Short Titles Act, 1896, and the Statute Law Revision Act, 1948.

Since 1963 the calendar year in which the Royal Assent was received forms an integral part of every short title, and is therefore given without a preceding comma. Capitalization should be given as in the short title section of each statute, which means that all words which are not conjunctions, prepositions or generalized terms like "other" and "etc." will be in capitals:

[1]Parliamentary and other Pensions
and Salaries Act 1976

It should, perhaps, be added that failure to observe the form of citation laid down in the short title sections of the statutes does not constitute an infringement of statutory law, as these sections are worded permissively (may) and not prescriptively (shall). For acts before 1963 it is correct to insert a comma before the date, as it is in apposition and not formally part of the short title:

[2]Acts of Parliament Numbering and Citation
Act, 1962

The date should always be added to the short title in this way, if not an integral part of it, because many statutes passed in different years have been given identical short titles, and the date is necessary to distinguish them.

There is, however, another method of identifying and distinguishing Acts of Parliament, and that is by their figurative position in the statute book according to their order of enactment. Since 1963 this mode of citation consists of the year the Royal Assent was received, and a chapter number according to the order in which the statutes received that assent. "Chapter" is abbreviated to "c.", and the number runs from 1 every year in arabic numerals:

[3]1970 c.48

It is not necessary to give chapter number with the short title of recent acts, unless in a table of statutes. If the short title is given in the textual matter (where it is not underlined), the year and chapter number may be given in a footnote. If both are cited together for some reason, the year and chapter number are enclosed in parentheses:

[4]Parliamentary and other Pensions and Salaries Act 1976 (1976 c.48)

It is quite common to omit the year from the parentheses when preceded by a short title with date:

[5]Parliamentary and other Pensions and Salaries Act 1976 (c.48)

Note that the "c." is never capitalized.

Up to the end of 1962 this form of citation was more complicated and often more essential. The chapter (or capitum) number was assigned to Acts in the order they received the Royal Assent during each Parliamentary session, indicated by the regnal years of the sovereign. This represented the inscribing of each new statute in turn as a new heading on the Parliamentary sessional rolls. Thus the Regency Act, 1953, was the first Act of Parliament to receive the Royal Assent from the session which began in November 1953, during the second year of the reign of Elizabeth II, and ended in November 1954 during her third regnal year. The citation then takes the form of the regnal years, linked by an ampersand, and a conventional abbreviation for the monarch, whose number is given in arabic form. The chapter number then follows a comma. The footnote reference is therefore:

[6] 2 & 3 Eliz.2, c.1

If the sovereign's name is abbreviated and immediately precedes the chapter number, the comma before the chapter number is deleted:

[7] Parliamentary Papers Act, 1840 (3 & 4 Vict. c.9) [Here the details have been added directly to the short title, so they are given in parentheses.]

It is advisable to add the date to the short title form as it is often difficult to translate regnal years. They vary for each sovereign because they commence with the date of accession to the throne. Though most Parliamentary sessions run over two regnal years, some may be limited to one regnal year:

[8] Diplomatic Privileges Act, 1708 (7 Anne, c.12)

and some sessions run on from one reign to the next:

[9] Cockfighting Act, 1952 (15 & 16 Geo.6 & 1 Eliz. 2, c.59)

If a second session of Parliament is held in a regnal year this is indicated by "sess. 2" in the citation:

[10] Trade Facilities and Loans Guarantee Act, 1922 (13 Geo.5, sess.2, c.5)

The first session is not specially indicated. Where a second or new Parliament is held in the same regnal year, the legislation of each of the Parliaments is treated as one statute (in fact all the acts of any Parliamentary session are theoretically one statute) and each statute is given a number, preceded by "st." for statute:

[11] Septennial Act, 1715 (1 Geo.1, st.2, c.38)

In this case "st. 1" would be specially indicated.

For Acts without a short title, regnal years form the only viable method of citation as the long titles of Acts are too cumbersome to use, often running to two or three lines of text. Where cited in isolation, the year may be added in parentheses:

[12] 18 & 19 Car.2, c.11 (1667)

A few Acts have developed conventional names which should be used:

[13] Lord Hardwicke's Act, 1753

Where several statutes concerning one topic have been enacted over a period of time, each extending and modifying the law concerning that topic, a collective short title may be assigned by the latest Act for convenient reference to the whole body of statutory law on that topic:

[14] Road Traffic Acts, 1930 to 1956

It is also sometimes necessary to cite an Act or some of its provisions together with its subsequent amendment by another Act:

[15] Trade Union and Labour Relation Act 1974, s.29(3) as amended by Trade Union and Labour Relation Act 1976, s.2

6:128   *Local Acts, Personal Acts and General Synod Measures.* Local Acts, Personal Acts, and General Synod Measures (the legislation of the established church: before 1971 called Church Assembly Measures) are cited in the same way as Public General Acts. Short titles, with the year added if not already present, should be used wherever possible. The only formal distinction is made in the chapter numbering where Local Acts are given a sequence of lower-case roman numerals:

[1] 25 & 26 Geo.5, c.xix

Personal Acts are given underlined arabic numerals:

[2] An Act for the better Regulation of Market Bosworth School, 1866 (29 & 30 Vict. c.8)

and General Synod Measures have "No." (Number) in place of chapter:

[3]Endowments and Glebe Measure 1976 (No.4)

As the underlining of arabic digits is not a very distinctive mark, it is permissible, indeed advisable, to add "(Personal Act)" after the number in place of underlining:

[4]29 & 30 Vict. c.8 (Personal Act)

6:129   *Sections of Acts.* Acts, particularly long ones, may be broken down into sections (given arabic numerals), sub-sections (indicated by arabic numerals in parentheses), paragraphs (lower-case roman letters in italics and parentheses), and sub-paragraphs (lower-case roman numerals in parentheses). They may be followed by Schedules, which are conventionally broken down into paragraphs and sub-paragraphs (with arabic numerals and arabic numerals in parentheses). Sometimes sections or Schedules may be broken down into parts, indicated by upper-case roman numerals. All of these features should be observed in citing sections, etc., of Acts. Sections are indicated by the abbreviation "s.", and further subdivisions only by their parentheses and numbering, except that italics are conventionally ignored:

[1]Companies Act, 1948, s.43(2)(d)(ii)

Schedules are indicated by "Sch.", and their paragraphs by "para.", but sub-paragraphs only by parentheses and numbering:

[2]British Library Act 1972, Sch.para.13
[3]Race Relations Act 1976, Sch.3 para.1(4)

6:130   *Bills.* Before Acts of Parliament receive the Royal Assent they are Parliamentary Bills, and their sections are called clauses, indicated by "c.". Bills may be introduced in either House and must go through a set procedure involving three readings and a Committee stage in both Houses. Bills should be cited by title, with the year of introduction added in parentheses:

[1]Channel Tunnel Bill (1974)

The stage that the Bill has reached should be indicated, since the text may vary through these stages, especially the second reading and the Committee stage:

[2] Cinematograph and Indecent Displays Bill (1973)
as amended by Standing Committee B, Commons.

[3] second reading, Lords

It will be seen that, as these stages are indistinguishable, the House is indicated.

It is not usual to distinguish a Commons Bill from a Lords Bill, but should this be necessary it can be done by adopting the numbering system used for Bills in the Sessional papers. The House of origination is indicated by "H.C. Bill" (or "H.L. Bill") followed by the years of the session, and a sequential arabic number within the session. Thus the Cinematograph and Indecent Displays Bill can be cited as:

[4] H.C. Bill 1973-74 [69]

If added directly to the Bill title it would be given in parentheses and the year of introduction would be omitted:

[5] Cinematograph and Indecent Displays Bill
(H.C. Bill 1973-74 [69])

Note that Commons Bills have their numbers enclosed in square brackets while Lords Bills numbers are given in parentheses:

[6] H.L. Bill 1973-74 (5)

It should be remembered that all Bills in progress are lost at the end of a Parliamentary session and if they are re-introduced in the next session they will be cited by the new session years and a new number.

Where the Bill subsequently becomes an Act of Parliament it is cited as the Bill for the Act, and the short title and date of the Act replace the title and date of the Bill:

[7] Bill for the Legal Aid and Advice Act, 1949

Individual clauses and sub-clauses, etc. can be shown in the same way as sections and sub-sections of Acts:

[8] c.1.3(2)

6:131 *Secondary legislation.* Secondary legislation consists of Statutory Instruments and, before 1948, Statutory Rules and Orders. These have official short titles and serial numbers given within each year. Citation should be by the authorized short title and date, followed by the serial identification to clarify the status of the title. The serial identification consists of the abbreviation "S.I." or "S.R. & O.", the year (which may differ from the short title date), and the number ("No."). This is in parentheses if attached to the short title, but not in parentheses if given separately:

> [1]Plant Breeders' Rights (Lupins) Scheme
> 1978 (S.I. 1978 No. 302)
> [2]S.I. 1978 No. 302
> [3]Statutory Instruments Regulations 1947
> (S.I. 1948 No.1)

Some Statutory Instruments are given additional codes according to whether they apply to Scotland, or to Northern Ireland, or to the administration of the courts. These codes may be given but they are not essential:

> [4]County Court (Amendment) Rules 1978
> (S.I. 1978 No. 682 (L.12))

Subdivisions of Instruments are cited according to the nature of the Instrument, as indicated in the short title. If called Rules or Regulations the subdivisions are referred to as rules and regulations, using the conventional abbreviation "r." (plural "rr."). If called an Order or Scheme the subdivisions are articles ("art." or "arts."). If they are specifically labelled as "Parts" in the Instrument they are indicated as "pt." (plural "pts."). Any further breakdown is given by the numbering and parentheses as for Acts:

> [5]National Galleries of Scotland Order 1978,
> art.3(1)(b) (S.I. 1978 No. 660 (S.60))

6:132 *Court cases.* Five elements are required to identify reports of court cases: the name of the case and the year, the volume number, the title and page number of the law report containing it.

The name of the case is given in the form of Plaintiff v. Defendant. Only the first name on each side is given and, for individuals, only the surname. The "v." is never spelt out as "versus" and it is read as "against" or "and". In textual matter the surnames are underlined but never the "v.". In Tables of cases the names are not underlined but the "v." is underlined. In footnotes none of the elements are underlined:

[1]Broome v. Speak   1903   1 Ch. 586, C.A.

If organizations are parties to a case their names are given in full, including forenames and initials, although abbreviations are used for such terms as Company and Limited and the ampersand is used instead of "and":

[2]Worcester Corsetry Ltd. v. Witting [1936] Ch.640

Titles of nobility are given in a brief form:

[3]R. v. Duke of Leinster [1924] 1 K.B. 311, C.C.A.

Where Latin phrases occur as part of the name of a case concerning a will or probate they should be retained. These are terms like "In re" or "Re", "In bonis" (abbreviated to "In b.") and "Ex parte" (abbreviated to "Ex p."). In textual citation these phrases are underlined, together with the names of the parties. In footnotes they should be underlined too, even though the names of the parties are not:

[4]In re Wilson v. Wilson, Ex p. Marum (1915) 84 L.J.K.B. 1893

[5]In re Gates, Arnold v. Gates [1933] 1 Ch. 913

In Criminal cases where prosecution is in the name of the Crown, Rex or Regina is abbreviated to "R.". If the Crown is party to Civil litigation, or respondent to a Criminal appeal, the English title is used without any abbreviation:

[6]Thomas v. The Queen (1874) 10 L.R.Q.B. 31

In appeals to the House of Lords the Director of Public Prosecutions is named as respondent in place of the Crown:

[7]R. v. Treacy [1970] 3 W.L.R. 592, C.A.; affirmed sub nom. Treasy v. D.P.P. [1971] A.C.537, H.L.

Information concerning appeal actions can be inserted in the citation, indicating if the original judgement was affirmed or reversed:

[8]Isaacs v. Chapman [1915] W.N. 415; affirmed [1916] W.N. 28

[9]Bowskill v. Dawson [1954] 1 Q.B. 288; reversed [1955] 1 Q.B. 13

Note that the name of the case can be inverted if the appeal is by the defendant. "Sub nomine" is used to explain the change of name and should be given in the citation in abbreviated form ("sub nom."):

[10]Boys v. Chaplin 1968 2 Q.B. 1, C.A.; affirmed sub nom. Chaplin v. Boys 1971 A.C.356, H.L.

6:133   *Date and law reports.* Modern series of law reports have their volume identified by year. Where two or three volumes are issued in the same year then the volume number must also be given in the citation. The date of the report is given in square brackets immediately after the name of the case. If necessary the volume number is then given before the title of the report. If the volume of the report series is identified by a number and not by a year, the date of the case decision is given in the same position, but in parentheses:

[1]Jones v. Robinson (1843) 11 M.& W. 758

Where the year of the law report is given, but is more than one year away from the date of the case decision, both years are given, with the decision date first:

[2]Thomas v. Cremin (1941) [1956] 1 W.L.R. 103, H.L.

Where an appeal is cited confirming or reversing the original decision, both dates should be given.

The title of the law report is given by conventional abbreviations, which are never underlined. They can be found in the sources already listed. The volume number precedes the title and the page number follows it. It is not necessary to cite more than one report of a case: the official report or a recognized report series should be cited. However, the

English Reports are cited in addition to other reports because this reprints most of the earlier nominate reports. It is conventional to cite the original report first, adding its location in the *English Reports* for the convenience of those who only have access to the reprint:

[3]Jones v. Robinson (1843) 11 M.& W. 758, 152 E.R. 1010

Where the only available report is in a textbook or a newspaper, the following form of citation should be followed:

[4]Beck v. Smirke (1894) as reported in Hudson, Law of building contracts (1914) ii, 259

[5]R. v. Vivian (1978) The Times, Aug.24, 14 col.2, C.A.

Many cases are not reported: though decisions are recorded in Court records, they are rarely of any great significance. Appeal cases are often of some interest, however, and transcripts of these are held by the Supreme Court Library (formerly the Bar Library) and may sometimes be cited. The fact that a case is unreported must be indicated, followed by a statement of where the record is kept. Though serial numbers were allocated by the Bar Library, they were often altered and do not contribute to the location of the case. They need not be cited:

[6]M. v. M. (1978, C.A.; unreported; Supreme Court Library) [Note that in this example the parties to the case have not been identified by the report. This is common practice in divorce and similar delicate Civil actions.]

Where the name of the report does not show the Court where the case was heard, it is possible though not essential, to add after the report and page number an abbreviation identifying the Court. This is useful where Appeal cases are cited in isolation, as the Court abbreviation shows that it is not a report of first instance proceedings.

[7][1894] A.C.202, H.L.

6:134 *Parliamentary publications.* Parliamentary debates, loosely referred to as "Hansard" though no longer a private service and officially titled *Parliamentary Debates: Official Report,* have been published in a number of series since their inception in 1803. The current series (the fifth) started in 1909 and publishes the Lords debates separately from the Commons debates. The form of citation is therefore volume number, an abbreviated title identifying the House, the series and the column number. The date should be added in parentheses for clarity:

[1]776 H.C.Deb. ser.5 col.380 (21 Jan. 1969)

Written answers, which are collected in a separate sequence at the end of each volume, may be distinguished by underlining the column number:

[2]776 H.C.Deb. ser.5 col.380 (30 Jan. 1969)

A preferable alternative for footnotes is to add "Written answer" in parentheses:

[3]776 H.C.Deb. ser.5 (Written answer 30 Jan. 1969)

The first four series published the debates of both Houses together and so are cited merely as Parliamentary Debates:

[4]37 Parl.Deb. ser.4 col.445 (17 Feb. 1896)

The official and permanent records of the proceedings of the two Houses, as distinct from the reporting of debates, are their Journals. These are cited similarly, by volume number, distinguishing abbreviation ("H.L.J." or "H.C.J.") and page number. Date should again be added in parentheses:

[5]207 H.C.J. 117 (4 Mar. 1952)

Command papers, supposedly presented to Parliament by Royal command, are numbered in series that run over several years. Each series is prefixed by an abbreviation, C. Cd. Cmd. and currently Cmnd. They should be cited by title (underlined in textual matter) and this should incorporate the name of the committee or other body responsible for the paper. Date of publication and serial number should be added in parentheses:

[6]Special Educational Needs. Report of the Committee of Enquiry into the Education of Handicapped Children and Young People (1978; Cmnd. 7212)

Where the responsible body is presented separately on the title page, it should be given first in the citation:

[7]Royal Commission on Gambling, Final report (1978; Cmnd. 7200) para.8.4

Commons papers and Lords papers, which are those called for by the Houses themselves, are cited in a similar fashion. These are numbered serially within each session in order of appearance. The Lords papers have their numbers in parentheses, the Commons papers do not. In citations the dates of the session should be given, the House abbreviation ("H.L." or "H.C."), and the sessional number; all in parentheses thus:

[8]Standing Committee B, Minutes of proceedings on the Policyholders Protection Bill (1974–75 H.C.651)

6:135   *Other official publications.* Official publications should, in general, be cited in the same way as other monographs. It is, however, conventional to cite well-known publications summarizing or explaining the law in certain fields by title and date alone. Such publications are frequently revised without any distinctive edition statement, so date of publication is the only possible distinguishing feature:

[1]The Highway Code (1978)

Official gazettes are cited by title without any abbreviation. The issue number and date of issue, which was often irregular, should be added:

[2]London Gazette no.6355 13–16 Mar. 1724 p.4

As can be seen from the last example, all these citations can include volume numbers and page numbers as for monograph citation, or refer to paragraphs and sub-paragraphs as appropriate.

6:136   *Books and periodicals.* Authors are cited by surname only, unless works are mentioned by more than one author with the same surname. The author's name is separated from the title of the work by a comma:

[1]Street, Principles of the Law of Damages (1962)

Joint authors' names are both given:

[2]Morris and Leach, The Rule against Perpetuities
(2nd ed. 1962) 31

A few traditional Common Law authorities like Blackstone's *Commentaries on the Laws of England* can be cited by using well-established abbreviations:

[3]Bl.Comm. (18th ed. 1829) ii 138

Where the author's name is incorporated into the title, e.g. *Craies on Statute Law*, it should be resolved into separate author and title elements:

[4]Craies, Statute Law (7th ed. 1971)

Note that all significant words in a title are capitalized and that the title is followed by statement of edition and date of publication given in parentheses. If required the surname of an editor or the number of a supplement may be added, separated by a comma, after the date:

[5]Archbold, Criminal Pleading, Evidence and
Practice (33rd ed. 1954, 12th supp. 1957)

[6]Geldart, Elements of English Law (5th ed. 1953,
rev. Hanbury)

Volume numbers are now given by lower-case roman numerals and page numbers by arabic numbers. The abbreviations "v." and "p." are not used:

[7]Holdsworth, A History of English Law (1938) xii,
235

Several volume and page citations may be given together:

[8]Pollock and Maitland, History of English Law
(2nd ed. 1971) ii, 501, iv, 301–305

If a work is part of a series, the title of the series, and number, if any, precede the date and are placed in parentheses:

[9]Encyclopedia of Highway Law and Practice
(Local Government Library) iii, para.6-101 (release 28:
8-10-74)

Many series have conventional abbreviations, such as the Selden Society publications:

¹⁰Hale, The Prerogatives of the King (S.S. XCII
1976, ed. Yale)

Periodical articles are cited by author's surname and title,
with the title enclosed in quotation marks. Then follows the
year in parentheses, the volume number, the title of the
periodical in abbreviated form, and page number:

¹¹Dwyer, "Immoral Contracts" (1977) 93 L.Q.R. 386

Reviews and similar "generic" titles or descriptions may be
similarly cited, but without the quotation marks:

¹²Wortley, Review (1977) 93 L.Q.R. 625

Articles or items within collections also have their titles
enclosed in quotation marks. The title and date of the
collection follow, using the conventions outlined above:

¹³Lepaulle, "Reflections on the Sources of the Law"
Essays in jurisprudence in honor of Roscoe Pound (1962,
ed. Newman) 90

Where the collection is the work of one author, the author's
surname is not repeated:

¹⁴Bentham, "Panopticon" Works (1893) iv, 122-24

6:137   *Loose-leaf services.* These are now a very common feature of
legal publication, especially in areas where the law is rapidly
changing such as taxation, planning and labour relations.
Such services are normally cited by the title without indicating
editors or publishers:

¹Social Welfare Law, para. D.471 (issue 0, April 77)

²Encyclopedia of Labour Relations Law ii, 2999/474
(release 39, 28-11-78)

However, if they are supplementary to a monograph the
conventions appropriate to books should be followed as far
as possible. Volume numbers should be given as for books,
and where any volume has a distinctive title of its own this
should be added:

³Kemp and Kemp, Quantum of Damages (4th ed. 1975)
ii, Personal Injury Reports, 1507 (release 8, 15-3-79)

Reference is usually given to paragraph number or page number, care being taken not to confuse the two if both are used by the same service. As the prime feature of loose-leaf services is the substitution of new pages bearing revised information for old pages of obsolete material it is impossible to assign a date to the service volume itself. Any issue numbering or dating system for the new inserts supplied by the service should, therefore, be added in parentheses after the paragraph or page numbers to which they relate, as in the above examples.

SECOND OR LATER REFERENCES

6:138   When a work has once been cited in complete form, later references to it are made in shortened forms. For these shortened titles or, where appropriate, the Latin abbreviation "ibid." should be used. The use of "op. cit." and "loc. cit.", formerly common in scholarly references, is no longer recommended.

"IBID."

6:139   When references to the same work follow each other without any intervening reference, even though the references are separated by several pages, the abbreviation "ibid." (for the Latin *ibidem*, "in the same place") is used to repeat as much of the preceding reference as is appropriate for the new entry:

[1]Max Plowman, An Introduction to the Study of Blake (London: Gollancz, 1952), p. 32. [A first, and therefore complete, reference to the work.]

[2]Ibid.
[With no intervening reference, a second mention of the same page of Plowman's work requires only "ibid." Notice that "ibid." is not underlined.]

[3]Ibid., p. 68.
[With no intervening reference since the last to Plowman's work, "ibid." is still correct, but here the reference is to a different page.]

6:140   Since "ibid." means "in the same *place*", it must not be used to repeat an author's name when references to two works by the same author follow each other without an intervening reference. Although repetition of the author's name in the second reference is the style preferred by many scholars, "idem" may be used. This Latin word, meaning "the same", is commonly used only in place of a person's name. It may be abbreviated to "id." if the abbreviation is consistently used. Do not confuse "ibid." and "idem": note that in footnote 2 "ibid." stands for *all* the items of the preceding reference except page number. "Idem", referring only to a person, should not be used here:

¹Arthur Waley, The Analects of Confucius (London: George Allen & Unwin, 1938), p. 33.

²Ibid., p. 38.

6:141   On the other hand, in the following examples, "ibid." in the second footnote is incorrect, since it is used to repeat only the author's name from the preceding footnote, all the other items being changed. "Idem", meaning the same person, is correct here.

¹Arthur Waley, The Analects of Confucius (London: George Allen & Unwin, 1938), p. 33.

Wrong:
²Ibid., Chinese Poems (London: George Allen & Unwin, 1946), p. 51.

¹Arthur Waley, The Analects of Confucius (London: George Allen & Unwin, 1938), p. 33.

Right:
²Idem, Chinese Poems (London: George Allen and Unwin, 1946), p. 51.

Repetition of the author's name would be equally correct; but, again, consistency is necessary.

Note that "idem" is a complete word, not an abbreviation, and is therefore not followed by a full stop.

6:142   If a number of pages separate references to a given work, the writer may prefer for the sake of clarity to repeat the title (in shortened form, when desired) rather than to use "ibid." even though no reference to another work has intervened.

SHORTENED REFERENCES

6:143   Reference to a work that has already been cited in full form, *but not in the reference immediately preceding*, is made in one of two styles, which shall be called method A and method B.

6:144   *Method A*. Method A uses the author's last name (but not the first name or initials unless another author of the same surname has been cited), the title (in shortened form, if desired) and the specific reference.

6:145   *For a book*, a second or later reference to a work already cited in full form, but not in the reference immediately preceding, *omits* the facts of publication, series title, if any, edition (unless more than one edition of the same work has been cited), and total number of volumes. Thus pared down, the reference consists of author's last name, title of the work, with page, and volume number as well, if necessary. Note the full reference in footnote 1 and a later reference to the work as shown in (arbitrarily numbered) footnote 9:

[1]Gabriel Marcel, The Mystery of Being, 2 vols. (Chicago: Henry Regnery Co., 1960), 1,42

[9]Marcel, Mystery of Being, 2,98-99

Now consider another multivolume work, which has an overall title and different titles for the individual volumes, only one of which is referred to in the notes:

[3]Albert C. Baugh, ed., A Literary History of England, vol. 2: The Renaissance (1500-1660), by Tucker Brooke (New York: Appleton-Century-Crofts, 1948), p. 104.

A later reference to Brooke's work should carry only the title of his single volume, not the title of the *multivolume work* or the volume number referring to it:

[9]Brooke, Renaissance, p. 130.

6:146   *For an article* in a magazine or journal, or for any component part of a work, such as a chapter in a book; or an essay, poem, or the like, in an anthology, a second or later reference to a work previously cited in its full form omits the name of the periodical, or book, or anthology, and omits also the volume number and date. The reference, then, consists of author's last name; title of the article, chapter, poem, essay (in shortened form, if desired) and page number. Examples of a full footnote reference to an article in a scholarly journal and its corresponding shortened form are shown in footnotes 4 and 7 below.

6:147   The following succession of footnotes illustrates the use of method A:

[1]Max Plowman, <u>An Introduction to the Study of Blake</u> (London: Gollancz, 1952), pp. 58-59.

[2]Plowman, note in William Blake's <u>The Marriage of Heaven and Hell</u>, reproduced in facsimile from an original drawing (London: J. M. Dent & Sons, 1927), pp. ix-xii. [Reference to another work by Plowman. The page numbers in small roman numerals are correct, since they are the style of numeral used in that part of the book containing Plowman's note.]

[3]Review of <u>An Introduction to the Study of Blake</u>, by Max Plowman, <u>Times Literary Supplement</u>, 8 June 1952, p. 12. [Reference to a popular magazine, which is identified by date alone. See para. 6:78.]

[4]Elspeth Longacre, "Blake's Conception of the Devil", <u>Studies in English</u> 90 (June 1937), 384. [This reference is to a scholarly journal, which is cited by both volume number and date. See para. 6:74.]

[5]Ibid. [The same as the reference immediately preceding.]

[6]Plowman, <u>Blake</u>, p. 125. [Reference to the first-noted work of Plowman, using the shortened title.]

[7]Longacre, "Blake's Devil", p. 381. [Another reference to Miss Longacre's journal article, using the shortened title. Other works having intervened since the complete reference in n. 4, "ibid." cannot be used.]

6:148   *Method B.* Method B uses the author's last name (without first name or initials unless another author of the same surname has been cited) and the page number (volume as well as page, if necessary). And this is all, unless more than one work by the same author has been cited previously, in which case the appropriate title (in shortened form, if desired) must be included in the reference. Works in which an association or institution or company stands as author must always include the title.

6:149   An example of a succession of footnotes illustrating the use of method B follows. It consists of the same works that are used to illustrate footnote practice under method A, thus pointing up the differences in the two methods:

[1]Max Plowman, An Introduction to the Study of Blake (London: Gollancz, 1952), pp. 58–59.

[2]Idem, note in William Blake's The Marriage of Heaven and Hell, reproduced in facsimile from an original drawing (London: J. M. Dent & Sons, 1927), pp. ix–xii. [Reference to another work by Plowman. Here "idem" is used to repeat the author's name. With no intervening reference, this is permissible (see para. 6:141). Note the small roman numerals used for page numbers, necessary in this case because the book itself so numbers its preliminary pages.]

[3]Review of An Introduction to the Study of Blake, by Max Plowman, Times Literary Supplement, 8 June 1952, p. 12. [Reference to a popular weekly periodical identified by date alone.]

[4]Elspeth Longacre, "Blake's Conception of the Devil", Studies in English 90 (June 1937), 384–88. [Reference to a scholarly journal identified by both volume and date.]

[5]Ibid. [The same as the reference immediately preceding.]

[6]Plowman, Blake, p. 125. [Since two works by Plowman have already been introduced, the title, here given in shortened form, is necessary.]

[7]Longacre, p. 381. [Another reference to Miss Longacre's article. Since only one work by her has been previously mentioned, the name and page number are sufficient under method B.]

SHORTENED TITLES

6:150   Generally speaking, titles of from two to five words need not be shortened, but length of the words may be considered and such a title as the following may be shortened as indicated:

129

Perspectives in American Catholicism   shortened to:
American Catholicism

6:151   A shortened title uses the key words of the main title,
omitting an initial "A", "An", or "The". Titles beginning
with such words as "A Dictionary of", "Readings in", "An
Index to", would normally omit those words, using the topic
as the short title:

A Guide to Rehabilitation of the Handicapped	Handicapped
Bibliography of North American Folklore and Folksong	Folklore and Folksong

There are, however, dictionaries and bibliographies that
cover a variety of topics: *An Index to General Literature,
Biographical, Historical, and Literary Essays and Sketches,
Reports and Publications of Boards and Societies Dealing
with Education.* It would not do to include but one category
in a short title; the only reasonable one is simply *Index.*

6:152   Following are examples of full titles with suitable
corresponding shortened titles:

FULL MAIN TITLE		SHORT TITLE
The Rise of the Evangelical Conception of the Ministry in America		Ministry in America
Classification and Identification of Handwriting		Handwriting
The American Dream of Destiny and Democracy	Or:	American Dream Destiny and Democracy
Creation Legends of the Ancient Near East		Creation Legends
"Blake's Conception of the Devil"		"Blake's Devil"

Neither the order of the words of the original title nor the
form of the words should be changed. *Creation Legends of
the Ancient Near East,* for example, should not be given the
short title *Near Eastern Legends.*

6:153   Normally, no part of a subtitle should be included in a shortened title. For such works as the following, the short titles come ready made: *The Pound Sterling: A History of English Money, Henry P. Davison: Biography.*

6:154   When a shortened title that might cause confusion is to be used, it is a convenience for the reader if the first full citation of the work notes that title (see para. 6:95).

CONTENT FOOTNOTES

6:155   Content (or substantive) footnotes consist of explanations or amplifications of the textual discussion and therefore resemble the text more than reference footnotes. When it is desirable to give the source of material included in a content footnote, the reference may be placed in one of several ways. It may be worked into a sentence, much as sources are sometimes worked into the text (see nn. 1, 2), or it may follow as a separate item (n. 3). In either case, whether the title is cited in full and whether the facts of publication are given depend upon whether the source has been referred to in a previous note:

[1]Detailed evidence of the great increase in the array of goods and services bought as income increases is shown in S. J. Prais and H. S. Houthaker, The Analysis of Family Budgets (Cambridge: Cambridge University Press, 1955), table 5, p. 52.

[2]Ernst Cassirer takes important notice of this in Language and Myth (pp. 59-62), and offers a searching analysis of man's regard for things on which his power of inspirited action may crucially depend. [Since the work has already been cited in full form, page reference only is required.]

[3]In 1962 the premium income received by all voluntary health insurance organizations in the United States was \$9.3 billion, while the benefits paid out were \$7.1 billion. Health Insurance Institute. Source Book of Health Insurance Data (New York: The Institute, 1963), pp. 36, 46.

[4]Professor D. T. Suzuki brings this out with great clarity in his discussion of "stopping" and "no-mindedness"; see, e.g., his chapter entitled

"Swordsmanship" in <u>Zen Buddhism and Its Influence on</u> <u>Japanese Culture</u> (Kyoto: Eastern Buddhist Society, 1938).

CROSS-REFERENCES

6:156   Occasionally a writer finds it necessary to refer to material in another part of his paper. Such references often consist simply of page or note numbers, or both, inserted in parentheses in the text. Cross-references may also appear in footnotes. The words "above" (earlier in the paper) and "below" (later in the paper) are frequently used with page or other cross-references because they make it clear that the reference is to the paper in hand, not to another source mentioned. ("Supra" and "infra" are sometimes used, chiefly in law references, in place of "above" and "below".)

6:157   The word "see" is often used with cross-references; "cf." should be used only in the sense of "compare" and is not an alternative for "see".

[1]For a detailed discussion of this matter see pp. 31-35 below.

6:158   A cross-reference such as "See n. 3 above", intended simply to refer to the title of a source, is not permissible; a shortened title, or "ibid.", should be used instead (see paras. 6:138–54).

7 Bibliographies

7:1   The rules for bibliographical style in this chapter and the examples of bibliographical entries in chapter 8 apply mainly to papers in literature, history, and other nonscientific fields. The style for lists of references accompanying scientific papers is explained in chapter 12. For typing bibliographies, see para. 13:37.

HEADING

7:2   The bibliography lists the sources used in writing the paper—not necessarily every work examined but those that were found relevant. The quoting of pertinent passages from works dealing primarily with subjects different from the subject of the paper does not alone warrant the inclusion of those works in the bibliography.

7:3   Since a bibliography rarely includes all that has been written upon a given topic, a more accurate heading for this section of the paper would be "Selected Bibliography", "Works Cited", or "Sources Consulted". The last is especially suitable if the list includes such sources as personal interviews, lectures, tape recordings, radio or television broadcasts, which for the sake of convenience are by common usage included in a bibliography.

CLASSIFICATION

7:4   Unless the bibliography is very short, it is usually classified, divided into sections. Among the more common schemes is that of division according to the types of source materials used; another is that of works by an author and works about

133

him; another, that of periods of time. There are many possible bases of classification, and the topic of the paper, its order of presentation, and its thesis will usually suggest the particular arrangement to be followed.

7:5   Sometimes the variety of source materials calls for further subdivision of the main classes, under second-level subheadings. Both levels of headings may be numbered or lettered.

7:6   Within the divisions and subdivisions, the entries should be arranged in a definite order. Although alphabetical order by surname of author is the most common, for some papers another order (for example, chronological, by date of publication) is more helpful. If a scheme other than alphabetical is used, it should be explained in a note either at the beginning of the bibliography or in a footnote on the first page of the bibliography.

BIBLIOGRAPHICAL ENTRIES COMPARED WITH FOOTNOTES

7:7   A bibliographical entry is similar to a full footnote reference in that it includes much the same material arranged in much the same order. Differences between the two in the way of presenting this material stem from the differences in purpose and placement. The purpose of the bibliographical entry is to list the work in full bibliographical detail: name(s) of author(s), full title of work, place, publisher, and date of publication. The purpose of the footnote, on the other hand, is primarily to inform the reader of the particular page, section, or other place from which the writer of the paper has taken certain material in his text. The secondary purpose of the footnote (to enable the reader to find the source for himself) dictates the inclusion of the full bibliographical details in the first reference to a work (see para. 6:13). The differences in style of presentation between footnotes and bibliography are described below (paras. 7:8–10) and illustrated by the parallel examples in chapter 8.

7:8   In a footnote, the author's full name is given in the natural order, first name first, because there is no reason to reverse the order; in the bibliographical entry, the surname is given first because bibliographies are usually arranged in alphabetical order by surnames of authors.

7:9   Where there are two or more authors' names, each is reversed in the bibliography, for consistency and because the surnames are more important (see examples in paras. 8:4–6). (An alternate style, used by some writers but not recommended here, is to reverse only the first name—in order to alphabetize the item—and to give the following names in normal order.)

7:10   Whereas commas and parentheses are used in a footnote, full stops are used in a bibliographical entry at the end of each main part—author's name, title of work, and facts of publication. Note, however, that references to periodicals usually retain the parentheses around the month and year when they follow the volume number (see examples in chap. 8).

7:11   Page numbers are listed in bibliographical entries only when the item is part of a whole work—a chapter in a book or an article in a periodical. When given, page numbers must be inclusive—first and last page of the relevant section (see paras. 6:82–83).

7:12   If the institution or department for which the paper is written requires a notation of the total number of pages for each book and pamphlet, the information is noted at the end of the entry: "Pp. xiv, 450."

ALPHABETIZING AUTHORS' NAMES

7:13   Family names containing particles vary widely both in capitalization and in form of alphabetization when arranged with surname first as in bibliographies and indexes. The preference of the bearer of the name (or tradition concerning it) as reflected in *Chambers's Bibliographical Dictionary*, should be followed in alphabetizing family names with particles. Note the wide variations in the following list:

à Beckett, Gilbert Abbott	Hindenburg, Paul von
Becket, Thomas à	La Fontaine, Jean de
Brink, Bernard ten	Van Der Goes, Hugo
de Gaulle, Charles	Van De Velde, Henri
De La Mare, Walter	Van Gogh, Vincent
de Vere, Aubrey Thomas	Von Wright, Georg Hendrik
De Vries, Hugo	

7:14   Names beginning with "Mc", "M'", or "Mac" should be alphabetized as though they all began with "Mac":

McAdam, John Loudon	M'Carthy, Justin
Macarthur, Mary Reid	MacCracken, Henry Noble
Macaulay, Rose	McCutcheon, John T.
McCarthy, Charles	Macdonald, Flora

7:15   Names beginning with "St" or "Ste" should be alphabetized as though they began with "Saint" or "Sainte". The name of a saint, however, should be alphabetized according to the personal name:

Augustine, Saint	Saint-Simon, Henri
Sainte-Beuve, Charles Augustin	

7:16   Compound surnames are alphabetized by the first name in the compound:

Watts-Dunton, Theodore
Lloyd George, David

7:17   Germanic names spelled with an umlaut are alphabetized as though "ä" were "ae", "ö" were "oe", and "ü" were "ue".

7:18   Spanish names which consist of given name (or names) and paternal name and maternal name joined with the conjunction *y* are alphabetized under the paternal name. Many names omit the conjunction, however, and in such a name as Manuel Ramón Albeniz, one does not know whether the father's surname is Ramón or whether it is a second given name. If the facts cannot be determined, the catalogue at your library may often serve as a guide.

7:19   A writer who has adopted a religious name sometimes writes under that name alone, preceded by the appropriate title.

Sometimes he adds his surname to the religious name. Alphabetize by the name rather than the title:

```
Eva Catherine, Sister        Hayden, Cuthbert, Father
```

7:20 Chinese and Arabic names are the chief non-Western names to cause problems in alphabetizing. In Chinese the family name precedes the given name and so the name is not reversed in alphabetizing:

```
Lin Yutang                   Mao Tse-tung
```

In Arabic, names beginning with *Abd, abu-,* or *ibn* are usually alphabetized under these elements; those beginning with *al-* ("the") are alphabetized by the element following this particle:

```
Abd-al-Hakam                 ibn-Khaldun
Gazali, al-
```

7:21 Authors with the same surname and the same first initial, one identified by initials alone, one by a single given name, and one by the same name plus a middle name, are alphabetized as follows:

```
Adams, J. B.
Adams, John
Adams, John Quincy
```

7:22 When reversed, names with "Sr" or "Jr" or a roman numeral are punctuated as follows:

```
Brownell, Arthur P., Jr
Edwards, Ira Raymond III
```

7:23 Works published under a pseudonym should be listed under the author's real name. The pseudonym may be enclosed in brackets and placed after the name if desired:

```
Baker, Ray Stannard [David Grayson]. Adventures
in Contentment.
```

Exceptions to this rule would be where authors are better known by their pseudonyms. Here the better known name would be used, the real name being added in brackets:

```
Carroll, Lewis [Charles Lutwidge Dodgson].
Alice's Adventures in Wonderland.
Eliot, George [Mary Ann Cross, née Evans].
Felix Holt.
Orwell, George [Eric Arthur Blair]. Animal Farm.
```

137

7:24   In a succession of works by the same author, the name is given for the first entry, and an eight-space line (the underlining key struck eight times) ending with a full stop takes its place in subsequent entries. The entries are arranged alphabetically by title or chronologically by date.

Tillich, Paul. <u>Love, Power, and Justice.</u>
New York: Oxford University Press, 1960.

————. <u>Systematic Theology</u>. 3 vols.
Chicago: University of Chicago Press, 1951-63.

7:25   Titles of works *edited* by the author or of works written by him in *collaboration* with others should not be alphabetized along with works written by him alone. In a list including all three categories, put the edited titles after the works written by the author in question, using an eight-space line for his name, followed by a comma and "ed."

7:26   The works of which he is a co-author follow the edited works, but the author's name must be repeated here. Do *not* use an eight-space line for a co-author's name, or to take the place of two or more co-authors.

7:27   A long bibliography of works by one man may carry a heading including his name, which would then not appear with each item. Works edited by him would either be under a subheading or begin with the abbreviation "Ed." Works he wrote in collaboration with others would begin, for example, "With Joseph P. Jones and John Q. Adams".

7:28   A work for which no author (editor, compiler, or other) is known appears in a bibliography under the title of the work, alphabetized by the first word, or the first word following an initial article.

TITLES OF WORKS

7:29   Capitalization of titles must agree with the scheme adopted for citing titles in footnotes and elsewhere in the paper (see paras. 4:5–12).

7:30   Underlining the titles of whole publications (books, periodicals, and all other works whose titles are underlined in footnotes and text) is optional in the bibliography, but the same style must be followed throughout the bibliography.

7:31   Quotation marks must be used around titles or articles and other component parts of whole publications (except in scientific papers; see chap. 12).

7:32   Foreign words and phrases in English titles must be underlined, except that titles entirely in a foreign language are not underlined if the option is taken of not underlining the titles of whole publications (see para. 7:30). A title in a foreign language that is enclosed in quotation marks is not underlined.

ANNOTATION

7:33   A bibliography may be annotated either in whole or in part. The annotation need not be a complete sentence grammatically, but it should begin with a capital and end with a full stop. The first line begins on the line following the entry proper and may be indented if desired:

```
Thompson, Oscar, ed. International Cyclopedia
    of Music and Musicians, New York: Dodd, Mead &
    Co., 1938.
        An admirable work which brings Grove up to
    date and deals adequately with contemporary
    music and American composers.
```

8 Sample Footnote References and Corresponding Bibliographical Entries

8:1 The following examples illustrate footnote and bibliographical forms exclusive of those used in citations of official publications (chap. 9) and in scientific fields (chap. 12).

8:2 The abbreviations "N." and "B." stand respectively for footnote entry and bibliographical entry.

BOOKS

8:3 *One author*

N. [1]Paul Tillich, Systematic Theology, 3 vols. (Chicago: University of Chicago Press, 1951-63), 1,9.

B. Tillich, Paul. Systematic Theology. 3 vols. Chicago: University of Chicago Press, 1951-63.

8:4 *Two authors*

N. [2]Walter E. Houghton and G. Robert Stange, Victorian Poetry and Poetics (Cambridge: Harvard University Press, 1959), p. 27.

B. Houghton, Walter E., and Stange, G. Robert. Victorian Poetry and Poetics. Cambridge: Harvard University Press, 1959.

8:5 *Three authors*

N. [3]Bernard R. Berelson, Paul F. Lazarsfeld, and William McPhee, Voting (Chicago: University of Chicago Press, 1954), pp. 93-95.

B. Berelson, Bernard R.; Lazarsfeld, Paul F.; and McPhee, William. Voting. Chicago: University of Chicago Press, 1954.

140

8:6   *More than three authors*

N.   [4]Jaroslav Pelikan et al., <u>Religion and the</u>
<u>University</u>, York University Invitation Lecture
Series (Toronto: University of Toronto Press,
1964), p. 109.

B.   Pelikan, Jaroslav; Ross, M. G.; Pollard, W.G.;
          Eisendrath, M. N.; Moeller, C.; and
          Wittenberg, A. <u>Religion and the University</u>.
          York University Invitation Lecture Series.
          Toronto: University of Toronto Press, 1964.

8:7   *No author given*

N.   [5]<u>The Lottery</u> (London: J. Watts, [1732]),
pp. 20-25.

B.   <u>The Lottery</u>. London: J. Watts, [1732].

8:8   *No author given; name supplied*

N.   [6][Henry K. Blank], <u>Art for Its Own Sake</u>
(Chicago: Nonpareil Press, 1910), p. 8.

B.   [Blank, Henry K.] <u>Art for Its Own Sake</u>.
          Chicago: Nonpareil Press, 1910.

8:9   *Pseudonymous author; real name supplied* (see paras.
6:20–22)

N.   [7]Elizabeth Cartright Penrose [Mrs
Markham]. <u>A History of France</u> (London: John
Murray, 1872), p. 9.

B.   Penrose, Elizabeth Cartright [Mrs Markham].
          <u>A History of France</u>. London: John Murray,
          1872.

8:10   *Institution, association, or the like, as "author"*

N.   [8]Special Libraries Association, <u>Directory</u>
<u>of Business and Financial Services</u> (New York:
Special Libraries Association, 1963), p. 21.

B.   Special Libraries Association. <u>Directory of</u>
          <u>Business and Financial Services</u>. New York:
          Special Libraries Association, 1963.

8:11   *Editor as "author" (same form used for compiler)*

N.   [9]J. N. D. Anderson, ed., <u>The World's</u>
<u>Religions</u> (London: Inter-Varsity Fellowship,
1950), p. 143.

B.   Anderson, J. N. D., ed. <u>The World's Religions</u>.
London: Inter-Varsity Fellowship, 1950.

8:12   *Author's work translated by another (same form if edited by
another)*

N.   [10]Ivar Lissner, <u>The Living Past</u>, trans.
J. Maxwell Brownjohn (New York: G. P. Putnam's
Sons, 1957), p. 58.

B.   Lissner, Ivar. <u>The Living Past</u>. Translated by
J. Maxwell Brownjohn. New York: G. P.
Putnam's Sons, 1957.

8:13   *Author's work contained in his collected works*

N.   [11]Samuel Taylor Coleridge, <u>The Complete
Works of Samuel Taylor Coleridge</u>, ed. W. G. T.
Shedd, Vol. 1: <u>Aids to Reflection</u> (New York:
Harper & Bros, 1884), p. 18.

B.   Coleridge, Samuel Taylor. <u>The Complete Works of
Samuel Taylor Coleridge</u>. Edited by W. G. T.
Shedd. Vol. 1: <u>Aids to Reflection</u>. New York:
Harper & Bros, 1884.

8:14   *Separately titled volume in a multivolume work with a general
title and editor*

N.   [12]Gordon N. Ray, gen. ed., <u>An Introduction to
Literature</u>, 4 vols. (Boston: Houghton Mifflin Co.,
1959), Vol. 2: <u>The Nature of Drama</u>, by Hubert
Hefner, pp. 47-49.

B.   Ray, Gordon N., gen. ed. <u>An Introduction to
Literature</u>. 4 vols. Boston: Houghton
Mifflin Co., 1959. Vol. 2: <u>The Nature of
Drama</u>, by Hubert Hefner.

8:15   *Separately titled volume in a multivolume work with a general
title and one author*

N.   [13]Will Durant, <u>The Story of Civilization</u>,
Vol. 1: <u>Our Oriental Heritage</u> (New York: Simon
& Schuster, 1942), p. 88.

B.   Durant, Will. <u>The Story of Civilization</u>. Vol. 1:
<u>Our Oriental Heritage</u>. New York: Simon &
Schuster, 1942.

8:16   *Book in a series*

N.   [14]Verner W. Clapp, <u>The Future of the
Research Library</u>, Phineas W. Windsor Series in

Librarianship, no. 8 (Urbana: University of
Illinois Press, 1964), p. 92.

B.   Clapp, Verner W. The Future of the Research
Library. Phineas W. Windsor Series in
Librarianship, no. 8. Urbana: University
of Illinois Press, 1964.

8:17   *Paperback series*

N.   [15]George F. Kennan, American Diplomacy,
1900-1950 (Chicago: University of Chicago Press,
1951; Phoenix Books, 1970), p. 48.

B.   Kennan, George F. American Diplomacy, 1900-1950.
Chicago; University of Chicago Press,
1951; Phoenix Books, 1970.

8:18   *Edition other than the first*

N.   [16]William R. Shepherd, Historical Atlas,
8th ed. (New York: Barnes & Noble, 1956), p. 62.

B.   Shepherd, William R. Historical Atlas. 8th ed.
New York: Barnes & Noble, 1956.

If the edition were edited by someone other than the author,
the edition number would be followed by the words "Edited
by . . . . "

8:19   *Reprint edition*

For a work that has been reprinted, it is important to give
publisher and date of the reprint following the usual
information about the book as originally issued:

N.   [17]Gunnar Myrdal, Population: A Problem for
Democracy (Cambridge: Harvard University Press,
1940; reprint ed., Gloucester, Mass.: Peter
Smith, 1956), p. 9.

B.   Myrdal, Gunnar. Population: A Problem for
Democracy. Cambridge: Harvard University
Press, 1940; reprint ed., Gloucester, Mass.:
Peter Smith, 1956.

8:20   *Title within a title*

A title of another work appearing within an underlined title is
enclosed in double quotation marks:

N.   [18]Arnold B. Come, <u>An Introduction to Barth's</u>
        <u>"Dogmatics" for Preachers</u> (Philadelphia:
        Westminster Press, 1963), pp. 90-92.

B.   Come, Arnold B. <u>An Introduction to Barth's</u>
        <u>"Dogmatics" for Preachers</u>. Philadelphia:
        Westminster Press, 1963.

8:21   When the title of a book occurs within a title that is in
quotation marks, such as the title of an article in a journal,
the book title is underlined:

N.   [19]Cedric H. Whitman. "Two Passages in the
        <u>Ion</u> of Euripides", <u>Classical Philology</u> 59
        (October 1964),257.

B.   Whitman, Cedric H. "Two Passages in the <u>Ion</u>
            of Euripides", <u>Classical Philology</u> 59
            (October 1964), 257-59.

8:22   When the title of an article appears within the title of another
article, single quotation marks are used:

"Comment on 'How to Make a Burden of the Public Debt'"

8:23   *Book with named author of introduction, preface, or
foreword*

N.   [20]Dag Hammarskjöld, <u>Markings</u>, with a
        Foreword by W. H. Auden (New York: Alfred
        A Knopf, 1964), p. 9.

B.   Hammarskjöld, Dag. <u>Markings</u>. Foreword by W. H.
            Auden. New York: Alfred A. Knopf, 1964.

If Auden's authorship of the foreword were more significant
than Hammarskjöld's book here, the following would be the
correct form:

N.   [21]W. H. Auden, Foreword to <u>Markings</u>, by
        Dag Hammarskjöld (New York: Alfred A. Knopf,
        1964), p. ix.

B.   Auden, W. H. Foreword to <u>Markings</u>, by Dag
            Hammarskjöld. New York: Alfred A. Knopf,
            1964.

8:24   *Book in a foreign language with English title supplied*

N.   [22]Maria Turlejska, <u>Rok przed kleska</u> |The
        year before the defeat| (Warsaw: Wiedza
        Powszechna, 1962), p. 445.

B.   Turlejska, Maria. Rok przed kleska [The year
        before the defeat]. Warsaw: Wiedza
        Powszechna, 1962.

Note that the English translation of the title is neither
underlined nor enclosed in quotation marks.

8:25   *Component part by one author in a work edited by another*

N.   [23]Paul Tillich, "Being and Love", in
        Moral Principles of Action, ed. Ruth N. Anshen
        (New York: Harper & Bros., 1952), p. 663.

B.   Tillich, Paul. "Being and Love". In Moral
        Principles of Action, pp. 661-72. Edited
        by Ruth N. Anshen. New York: Harper &
        Bros., 1952.

8:26   *Book privately printed*

N.   [24]John G. Barrow, A Bibliography of
        Bibliographies in Religion (Austin, Tex.:
        By the Author, 716 Brown Bldg., 1955), p. 25.
        [Street address not always given.]

B.   Barrow, John G. A Bibliography of Bibliographies
        in Religion. Austin, Tex.: By the Author,
        716 Brown Bldg., 1955.

8:27   *Secondary source of quotation*

N.   [25]Jesuit Relations and Allied Documents,
        vol. 59, n. 41, quoted in [or "cited by"]
        Archer Butler Hulbert, Portage Paths (Cleveland:
        Arthur H. Clark, 1903), p. 181.

B.   Jesuit Relations and Allied Documents, vol. 59,
        n. 41. Quoted in (or "cited by") Archer
        Butler Hulbert, Portage Paths, p. 181.
        Cleveland: Arthur H. Clark, 1903.

REPORTS—PUBLISHED

8:28   *Author named*

N.   [1]John H. Postley, Report on a Study of
        Behavioral Factors in Information Systems
        (Los Angeles: Hughes Dynamics, [1960]), p. 15.

B.   Postley, John H. Report on a Study of Behavioral
        Factors in Information Systems. Los
        Angeles: Hughes Dynamics, [1960].

8:29   *Chairman of committee named*

N.   [2]Report of the Committee on Financial
Institutions to the President of the United
States, by Walter W. Heller, Chairman (Washington,
D.C.: Government Printing Office, 1963), p. 12.

B.   Report of the Committee on Financial Institutions
to the President of the United States.
By Walter W. Heller, Chairman. Washington,
D.C.: Government Printing Office, 1963.

8:30   For reports published in microform see para. 8:42.

PROCEEDINGS—PUBLISHED

8:31   N.   [1]Industrial Relations Research Association,
.Proceedings of Third Annual Meeting (Madison,
Wis.: n.p., 1951), p. 30. [The date of the
meeting is often part of the title.]

B.   Industrial Relations Research Association.
Proceedings of Third Annual Meeting.
Madison, Wis.: n.p., 1951.

UNPUBLISHED REPORTS AND PROCEEDINGS

8:32   Titles of unpublished reports and proceedings are enclosed in
quotation marks. When not given in the title, place and date
follow it. There may also be the notation "Typewritten" or
"Mimeographed" in parentheses (see para. 8:45).

YEARBOOKS

8:33   *Department of government*

N.   [1]United States, Department of Agriculture,
Yearbook of Agriculture, 1941 (Washington, D.C.:
Government Printing Office, 1941), p. 683.

B.   United States, Department of Agriculture,
Yearbook of Agriculture, 1941. Washington,
D.C.: Government Printing Office, 1941.

8:34   *Article in a yearbook*

N.   [2]G. M. Wilson, "A Survey of the Social
and Business Use of Arithmetic", Second Report

of the Committee on Minimal Essentials in
<u>Elementary-School Subjects</u>, in <u>Sixteenth</u>
<u>Yearbook of the National Society for the Study</u>
<u>of Education</u>, pt. 1 (Bloomington, Ill.: Public
School Publishing Co., 1917), pp. 20-22.

B.   Wilson, G. M. "A Survey of the Social and
Business Use of Arithmetic." <u>Second Report</u>
<u>of the Committee on Minimal Essentials in</u>
<u>Elementary-School Subjects</u>, in <u>Sixteenth</u>
<u>Yearbook of the National Society for the</u>
<u>Study of Education</u>, pt. 1. Bloomington,
Ill.: Public School Publishing Co., 1917.

ARTICLES IN JOURNALS OR MAGAZINES

8:35   *Article in a journal*

N.   [1]Don Swanson, "Dialogue with a Catalogue",
<u>Library Quarterly</u> 34 (December 1963),115.

B.   Swanson, Don. "Dialogue with a Catalogue",
<u>Library Quarterly</u> 34 (December 1963),
113-25.

See paragraph 6:74. In citing journals that are numbered only
by issue, not volume, note the style set forth in paragraph
6:76; and journals that publish volumes in successive series,
numbered or lettered, paragraph 6:77.

8:36   *Article in a magazine*

N.   [2]Barbara W. Tuchman, "If Asia Were Clay
in the Hands of the West", <u>Atlantic</u>, September
1970, p. 72.

B.   Tuchman, Barbara W. "If Asia Were Clay in the
Hands of the West", <u>Atlantic</u>, September
1970, pp. 68-84.

(See also para. 6:78.)

ARTICLES IN ENCYCLOPAEDIAS

8:37   *Signed article*

N.   [1]<u>Encyclopaedia Britannica</u>, 11th ed., s.v.
"Blake, William," by J. W. Comyns-Carr.

B.   Encyclopaedia Britannica, 11th ed. S.v. "Blake,
     William," by J. W. Comyns-Carr.

8:38   *Unsigned article*

N.   ²Encyclopedia Americana, 1963 ed., s.v.
        "Sitting Bull".

B.   Encyclopedia Americana, 1963 ed. S.v. "Sitting
     Bull".

(See also paras. 6:101, 8:39.)

NEWSPAPERS

8:39   N.   ¹San Francisco Chronicle, 5 June 1971.

Bibliographical entry is the same in this case, but see
paragraph 8:40.

N.   ²"Amazing Amazon Region", New York Times,
        12 January 1969, sec. 4, p. E11.

B.   "Amazing Amazon Region", New York Times,
     12 January 1969, sec. 4, p. E11.

Several matters to be considered in referring to newspapers
are discussed in paragraphs 6:97–100.

8:40   In the bibliographical entries shown for journal, magazine,
encyclopaedia, and newspaper articles, the style assumes in
each case only one reference to the publication. If the writer
has used the issues of a periodical covering a considerable
period of time, this fact may be indicated by giving the title of
the periodical with the dates as in notes 1 or 2, as may be
appropriate:

¹Saturday Review, 2, 16, 30 July; 2, 20, 27
August 1966.
²Times, 4 January–6 June 1964.

Two or more articles in an encyclopaedia or similar reference
work may be contained in one bibliographical entry:

Columbia Encyclopedia, 3rd ed. (1963). S.v.
    "Custer, George Armstrong", "Sioux
    Indians".

Several articles in the same magazine or professional journal should always be listed separately, each under its author.

BOOK REVIEWS

8:41 N. [1]Benjamin De Mott, review of <u>Briefing for</u> <u>a Descent into Hell</u>, by Doris Lessing, in <u>Saturday Review</u>, 13 March 1971, p. 25.

B. De Mott, Benjamin. Review of <u>Briefing for a</u> <u>Descent into Hell</u>, by Doris Lessing. <u>Saturday Review</u>, 13 March 1971, pp. 25-26.

MICROFORM REPRODUCTIONS

8:42 N. [1]Godwin C. Chu and Wilbur Schramm. <u>Learning from Television: What the Research Says</u> (Bethesda, Md.: ERIC Document Reproduction Service, ED 014 900, 1967), p. 3.

B. Chu, Godwin C., and Schramm, Wilbur. <u>Learning</u> <u>from Television: What the Research Says</u>. Bethesda, Md.: ERIC Document Reproduction Service, ED 014 900, 1967.

(See also para. 6:118.)

UNPUBLISHED MATERIALS

MANUSCRIPT COLLECTIONS

8:43 An individual document in a manuscript collection, like a page in a book, may be referred to in a footnote but seldom appears in a bibliography. If mentioned, it should be the last item in the bibliographical entry, rather than the first as in the footnote:

N. [1]Gen. Joseph C. Castner, "Report to the War Department", 17 January 1927, Modern Military Records Division, Record Group 94, National Archives, Washington, D.C.

B. Washington, D.C. National Archives. Modern Military Records Division. Record Group 94. Gen. Joseph C. Castner, "Report to the War Department", 17 January 1927.

N. [2]Stimson Diary and War Letters, February 1918, Henry L. Stimson Papers, Yale University, New Haven, Conn.

149

    B.   New Haven, Conn. Yale University. Henry L.
        Stimson Papers.

    N.   [3]British Museum, Arundel MSS, 285,
        fol. 165b.

    B.   London, British Museum. Arundel MSS.

8:44   Note that the title of a document is enclosed in quotation marks, but that such general designations as *diary, letter, memorandum* are capitalized but neither quoted nor underlined in footnote and bibliographical entries. (See also para. 6:119.)

THESES AND OTHER PAPERS

8:45   Note that "unpublished" is not included in the designation, the title within quotation marks indicating that the work is not published:

    N.   [1]O. C. Phillips, Jr., "The Influence of
Ovid on Lucan's <u>Bellum civile</u>" (Ph.D. dissertation, University of Chicago, 1962), p. 14.

    B.   Phillips, O. C., Jr. "The Influence of Ovid on
        Lucan's <u>Bellum civile</u>". Ph.D. dissertation,
        University of Chicago, 1962.

    N.   [2]American Institute of Planners, Chicago
Chapter, "Regional Shopping Centres Planning Symposium", Chicago, 1942. (Mimeographed.)

    B.   American Institute of Planners, Chicago Chapter.
        "Regional Shopping Centers Planning
        Symposium." Chicago, 1942. (Mimeographed.)

    N.   [3]H. P. Luhn, "Keyword-in-Context Index for
Technical Literature", paper presented at the 136th meeting of the American Chemical Society, Atlantic City, N.J., 14 September 1959.

    B.   Luhn, H. P. "Keyword-in-Context Index for
        Technical Literature". Paper presented at
        the 136th meeting of the American Chemical
        Society, Atlantic City, N.J., 14 September
        1959.

    N.   [4]Morristown (Kansas) Children's Home,
Minutes of Meetings of the Board of Managers, 1945-55, meeting of 6 May 1950. (Typewritten.)

B.   Morristown (Kansas) Children's Home. Minutes of
Meetings of the Board of Managers, 1945-55.
(Typewritten.)

MULTIPLE REFERENCES CONTAINED IN A SINGLE FOOTNOTE

8:46   The individual references in a footnote citing several works
are separated with semicolons:

N.   [1]See Samuel P. Langley, James Smithson
(Washington, D.C.: Smithsonian Institution,
1904), pp. 18, 19; Paul Oehser, Sons of Science
(New York: Henry Schuman, 1949), pp. 1, 9-11;
and Webster True, The First Hundred Years of
the Smithsonian Institution: 1846-1946 (Washington, D.C.: Smithsonian Institution, 1946),
p. 2.

The bibliographical entries would be alphabetized separately:

B.   Langley, Samuel P. James Smithson. Washington,
D.C.: Smithsonian Institution, 1904.

B.   Oehser, Paul. Sons of Science. New York:
Henry Schuman, 1949.

B.   True, Webster. The First Hundred Years of the
Smithsonian Institution: 1846-1946.
Washington, D.C.: Smithsonian Institution,
1946.

INTERVIEWS

8:47   Since interviews may be of considerable value as sources, they
may be included in a bibliography, even though they are not
written material.

N.   [1]Interview with John Nought, Primus Realty
Company, San José, California, 12 May 1962.

B.   Nought, John. Primus Realty Company, San José,
California. Interview, 12 May 1962.

9   Official Publications

9:1   The form used for citing official publications should be one that makes them readily accessible to anyone wishing to locate them in a library. The arrangement of information on the title pages of the documents themselves, its amount, and its complexity raise puzzling questions of how much of the information it is necessary to include and in what order it should be set down in the footnote. Here reference to the catalogue at your library can be of great help, although it is not a safe guide in such matters as capitalization and punctuation of titles, which for official publications as well as for other references must follow the scheme of the paper. When in doubt of how much to include in a reference, it is better to err on the side of giving too much rather than too little information.

9:2   The name of the country, county, state, city, town, or other government district (e.g., United Kingdom, United States, Surrey, Illinois, Liverpool, Baltimore) is given first in the citation of an official publication issued by one of them or under its auspices. Then comes the name of the legislative body, court, executive department, bureau, board, commission, or committee. The name of the office rather than the title of the officer should be given except where the title of the officer is the only name of the office, as, for example, "Illinois, State Entomologist". The name of the division, regional office, etc., if any, follows the name of the department, bureau, or commission. Thus the "author" of a document might read: United Kingdom. Department of

Employment. Solicitors Office. Following the name of the author, the title of the document, if any, should be given. From this point, the information noted is dependent largely upon the nature of the material.

9:3   Generally speaking, references to official publications do not include the facts of publication. When, however, the document has a personal author whose name is included (as it should be) in the reference, it is best to show the facts of publication. For some such references the date of publication may be the only clue to the date of the work (see para. 9:7, n. 5).

BRITISH GOVERNMENT DOCUMENTS[1]

9:4   Citations to British government documents should begin with the name of the authorizing body under which they were issued—Parliament, Public Record Office, Foreign Office, Ministry of Transport, and so on, always preceded by "United Kingdom".

9:5   Under the provision of the *Acts of Parliament Numbering and Citation Act* of 1962 statutes are cited by year and a serial number, a running number for the year called the chapter number, thus

```
United Kingdom. Laws, Statutes, etc.,
    Iron and Steel Act, 1967, ch.17.

United Kingdom. Laws, Statutes, etc.,
    Consolidated Fund Act, 1963, ch.1.
```

English statutes prior to January 1963 are always cited by name, regnal year of the sovereign, and chapter number. Names of sovereigns are abbreviated and arabic numerals are used throughout the references. Before publication in the *Statutes* or in the *Public General Acts and Church Assembly*

---

[1]For a description of the various kinds of British government documents, see the current edition of John E. Pemberton's *British Official Publications* (Pergamon Press).

Measures, statutes are cited as in note 1; when they are published in one or the other compilation, their citations follow the forms of notes 2 and 3:

N. [1]United Kingdom, Laws, Statutes, etc., Coroner's Act, 1954, 2 & 3 Eliz. 2, ch. 31.

B. United Kingdom. Laws, Statutes, etc. Coroner's Act, 1954, 2 & 3 Eliz. 2, ch. 31.

N. [2]United Kingdom, Laws, Statutes, etc., Transport Act, 1962, 10 & 11 Eliz. 2, ch. 46, Halsbury's Statutes of England (2nd ed.), 42, 565-68 (pt. 1, sec. 3-6).

B. United Kingdom. Laws, Statutes, etc. Transport Act, 1962, 10 & 11 Eliz. 2, ch. 46. Halsbury's Statutes of England (2nd ed.), vol. 42.

N. [3]United Kingdom, Laws, Statutes, etc., Trustee Savings Banks Act, 1964, 12 Eliz. 2, ch. 4, Public General Acts and Church Assembly Measures, 1964, pt. 1, p. 6 (sec. 2/3).

B. United Kingdom. Laws, Statutes, etc., Trustee Savings Banks Act, 1964. 12 Eliz. 2, ch. 4, Public General Acts and Church Assembly Measures, 1964, pt. 1.

9:6 The *Parliamentary Papers* are bound annually in consecutive volumes of *Bills, Reports,* and *Accounts and Papers.* Each of these has its own series of volume numbers, which means that any one title is, for example, volume 2 in its own series and volume 10 of the *Parliamentary Papers* for the year. In the volumes of *Reports,* the separate, individually paged documents are arranged alphabetically by their subjects. The three series are composed of "command" papers and are cited as such (n. 1 below), with number and title, if desired:

N. [1]United Kingdom, Parliament, Parliamentary Papers (Commons), 1962-63, vol. 19 (Reports, vol. 8), Cmnd. 2062, December 1962, "Report of the Ministry of Health for the Year Ended 31 December 1962," ch. 2, pp. 8-10 [of the report].

B. United Kingdom. Parliament. Parliamentary Papers (Commons), 1962-63, vol. 19 (Reports, vol. 8). Cmnd. 2062, "Report of the Ministry of Health for the Year Ended 31 December 1962".

9:7   The *Sessional Papers* (not to be confused with the *Parliamentary Papers*, which also are sometimes referred to as *Sessional Papers*) have been published since 1938–39 following each session of Parliament separately for the two houses. The series is divided into eight titles—five for the House of Commons and three for the House of Lords. The annual series of *Papers* is identified by year date alone, but each of the eight titles has its individual set of volume numbers. A citation to these *Sessional Papers* can be deceiving, since some of the volumes are made up of separate papers that are individually paged and arranged either chronologically by day or alphabetically by subject. Citations should be made, not to page numbers, but to the specific document by its title, with pertinent numbered sections or paragraphs if the paper is long. The books have well-arranged tables of contents and indexes, and locating a particular paper is no problem. (See nn. 1 and 2, below.)

N.   [1]United Kingdom, Parliament, Sessional Papers (Commons), 1962–63, Votes and Proceedings, 19 March 1963, "Navy Supplementary Estimate, 1962–63" (Supply). |No volume number in this case, since there was but one in 1962–63. The arrangement is alphabetical by subject, "Supply".|

B.   United Kingdom. Parliament. Sessional Papers (Commons), 1962–63. Votes and Proceedings, 19 March 1963, "Navy Supplementary Estimate, 1962–63" (Supply).

N.   [2]United Kingdom, Parliament, Sessional Papers (Lords), 1962–63, Public Bills, vol. 1, "Contracts of Employment", sec. 2.

B.   United Kingdom. Parliament. Sessional Papers (Lords), 1962–63. Public Bills, vol. 1, "Contracts of Employment".

9:8   Since 1909 the *Parliamentary Debates* have been published separately for the two houses. The name *Hansard* (for the original printer of the *Debates*) is properly omitted from the title of volumes issued since 1891, but it still has official sanction and is sometimes used even now (n. 2). Both series and volume numbers are necessary:

N.   [1]United Kingdom, Parliament, Parliamentary Debates (Commons), 5th series, 721 (1965), 779–87.

> B.   United Kingdom. Parliament. <u>Parliamentary Debates</u> (Commons), 5th series, <u>vol.</u> 721 (1965).
>
> N.   ²United Kingdom, Parliament, <u>Hansard's Parliamentary Debates</u> (Lords), 5th series, 58 (1924),11-15
>
> B.   United Kingdom. Parliament. <u>Hansard's Parliamentary Debates</u> (Lords), 5th series, vol. 58 (1924).

9:9 The *British Foreign and State Papers* are arranged within the volumes alphabetically by country and, further, by subject:

> N.   ¹United Kingdom, Foreign Office, <u>British Foreign and State Papers</u>, 1852-53, "Austria: Proclamation of the Emperor Annulling the Constitution of 4th March, 1849", 41, 1298-99.
>
> B.   United Kingdom. Foreign Office. <u>British Foreign and State Papers, 1852-53,</u> "Austria: Proclamation of the Emperor Annulling the Constitution of 4th March, 1849", vol. 41.

9:10 Reports are issued in pamphlet form by the several ministries, commissions, committees, and the like:

> N.   ¹United Kingdom, Office of the Minister of Science, Committee on Management and Control of Research, <u>Report, 1961</u>, p. 58.
>
> B.   United Kingdom. Office of the Minister of Science. Committee on Management and Control of Research. <u>Report, 1961</u>.

9:11 The early records entitled *Calendar of . . .* are arranged chronologically. In some, numbered items (grants, leases, warrants, pardons, and so on) appear within a "calendar" of no uniform duration (n. 1). Dates are essential, therefore, in identifying the items:

> N.   ¹United Kingdom, Public Record Office, <u>Calendar of the Patent Rolls</u>, Eliz. [1], vol. 4 (1566--69): Calendar 66 (17 November 1566--16 November 1567), 2 May 1567, no. 455, Pardon for Richard Byngham, pp. 63-64.
>
> B.   United Kingdom. Public Record Office. <u>Calendar of the Patent Rolls</u>, Eliz. [1], vol. 4 (1566-69), Calendar 66: 2 May 1567, no.455.

N.   [2]United Kingdom, Public Record Office,
            Calendar of State Papers, Domestic, of the Reign
            of Charles 2, vol. 209 (1667), 12 July 1667,
            Earl of Carlisle to Williamson, p. 289.

B.   United Kingdom. Public Record Office. Calendar
            of State Papers, Domestic, of the Reign
            of Charles 2, vol. 209 (1667), 12 July
            1667, Earl of Carlisle to Williamson.

N.   [3]United Kingdom, Public Record Office, Calendar
            Calendar of Treasury Books, vol. 32 (1718),
            pt. 2: 27 February, "Royal Warrant to the Clerk
            of the Signet. . . ."

B.   United Kingdom, Public Record Office. Calendar
            of Treasury Books, vol. 32 (1718), pt. 2:
            27 February, "Royal Warrant to the Clerk
            of the Signet. . . ."

N.   [4]United Kingdom, Public Record Office,
            List and Analysis of State Papers, Foreign
            Series, Eliz. [1] (1 August 1589—30 June 1590),
            vol. 1: III, Spain, no. 637, "Spanish Agents
            in England".

B.   United Kingdom. Public Record Office. List and
            Analysis of State Papers, Foreign Series,
            Eliz. [1] (1 August 1589--30 June 1590),
            vol. 1: III, Spain, no. 637.

UNITED STATES GOVERNMENT DOCUMENTS

9:12 The United States government publishes its official documents in two main categories—those originating in the Congress and those originating in the executive departments.

CONGRESSIONAL DOCUMENTS

9:13 The proceedings of each house of Congress, together with the presidential messages to it, are published in the *Journal*, separately for House and Senate, at the close of each session. The debates appear in the *Congressional Record* (since 1873). Besides the bills and resolutions initiated by the Congress, there are the materials furnished to it by committees, governmental agencies, and executive officers of government—reports, hearings, miscellaneous documents.

Citations to all of them must include, in addition to the authorizing body, the number, session, and date of the Congress; title and number (if any) of the document; and, in some instances, the title of the work in which the document can be found, with relevant volume and page number(s).

9:14   The letters "N." and "B." stand, respectively, for footnote entry and bibliographical entry.

9:15   *Bills, reports, and miscellaneous documents*

N.   [1]United States, Congress, House, <u>A Bill to Require Passenger-Carrying Motor Vehicles Purchased for Use by the Federal Government to Meet Certain Safety Standards</u>, H.R. 1341, 86th Cong., 1st sess., 1959, pp. 1-4

B.   United States. Congress. House. <u>A Bill to Require Passenger-Carrying Motor Vehicles Purchased for Use by the Federal Government to Meet Certain Safety Standards</u>. H.R. 1341, 86th Cong., 1st sess., 1959.

N.   [2]United States, Congress, Senate, <u>Planning in Metropolitan Areas</u>, S. Rept. 821 to Accompany S. 855, 88th Cong., 2nd sess., 1963, pp. 3-5.

B.   United States. Congress. Senate. <u>Planning in Metropolitan Areas</u>, S. Rept. 821 to Accompany S. 855, 88th Cong., 2nd sess., 1963.

N.   United States, Congress, Senate, <u>Report of the Federal Trade Commission</u>, S. Doc. 92, 70th Cong., 1st sess., 1935, pt. 71A.

B.   United States. Congress. Senate. <u>Report of the Federal Trade Commission</u>, S. Doc. 92, 70th Cong., 1st sess., 1935.

N.   [4]United States. Congress, Senate. Committee on Foreign Relations, <u>Technical Assistance and Related Programs</u>. S. Rept. 1956, 84th Cong., 2nd sess., 1960, <u>Senate Miscellaneous Reports on Public Bills</u> 3, 184-85.

B.   United States, Congress, Senate, Committee on Foreign Relations. <u>Technical Assistance and Related Programs</u>. S. Rept. 1956, 84th Cong., 2nd sess., 1960. <u>Senate Miscellaneous Reports on Public Bills</u>, vol. 3.

N.   [5]United States, Congress, Joint Economic Committee,

The Low-Income Population and Economic Growth,
by Robert J. Lampman, Joint Committee Print,
Study Paper 12 (Washington, D.C.: Government
Printing Office, 1959), pp. 14-15.

B.   United States Congress. Joint Economic Committee.
The Low-Income Population and Economic
Growth, by Robert J. Lampman. Joint
Committee Print, Study Paper 12, Washington,
D.C.: Government Printing Office, 1959.

N.   [6]United States, Congress, House, The Drug
Abuse Control Amendments of 1965, 89th Cong., 1st
sess., 1965, Journal, 10 March 1965, pp. 337-42.

B.   United States. Congress. House. The Drug Abuse
Control Amendments of 1965. 89th Cong., 1st
sess., 1965. Journal, 10 March 1965.

9:16   Hearings should be cited by title. If the "author" does not
indicate the committee before whom the hearings were held,
the committee should be named in the reference.

N.   [7]United States, Congress, House, Committee on
Ways and Means, Narcotics, Marihuana, and Barbi-
turates, Hearings before a subcommittee of the
House Committee on Ways and Means on H. R. 3490,
82nd Cong., 1st sess., 1951, p. 4.

B.   United States. Congress. House. Committee on Ways
and Means. Narcotics, Marihuana, and Barbi-
turates. Hearings before a subcommittee of
the House Committee on Ways and Means on
H.R. 3490, 82nd Cong., 1st sess., 1951.

9:17   Congressional bills and resolutions are published in pamphlet
form. When a bill is enacted into law, it becomes a part of the
Statutes at Large. In the interim between its having been
introduced into one of the houses and its passage and
publication as a law in the *Statutes,* a bill is cited to the slip
bill, or to the *Congressional Record* if it is contained therein:

N.   [8]United States, Congress, House, An Act to Amend
the Bank Holding Company Act of 1956, Pub. L.
89-485, 89th Cong., 2nd sess., 1966, H.R. 7371,
p. 3

B.   United States. Congress. House. An Act to Amend the
Bank Holding Company Act of 1956. Pub. L.
89-485, 89th Cong., 2nd sess., 1966, H.R. 7371.

9:18   Congressional debates are printed in the *Congressional Record*. Unless the subject of the speech, or merely of the remarks, is mentioned in the text, it is proper to include it in the citation:

N.   [9]United States, Congress, Senate, Senator Blank speaking for the Amendment of the Standing Rules of the Senate, S. Res. 103, 89th Cong., 1st sess., 14 November 1965, Congressional Record 102,6522. |A reference to the bound volume, which is differently paged from the Daily Digest.|

B.   United States. Congress. Senate. Senator Blank speaking for the Amendment of the Standing Rules of the Senate. S. Res. 103, 89th Cong., 1st sess., 14 November 1965. Congressional Record, vol. 102.

9:19   Presidential proclamations, executive orders, and any other documents submitted by the president, or orders to be published, are carried in the *Federal Register*, which is issued on every day following a government working day:

N.   [10]United States, President, Proclamation, "Supplemental Quota on Imports of Long-Staple Cotton," Federal Register 15, no. 196, 10 October 1950, 6801-2.

B.   United States. President. Proclamation. "Supplemental Quota on Imports of Long-Staple Cotton." Federal Register 15, no. 196, 10 October 1950, 6801-2.

9:20   The public papers of the presidents of the United States are collected in two large works:

N.   [11]J. D. Richardson, ed., Compilation of the Messages and Papers of the Presidents, 1789-1897. 53rd Cong., 2nd sess., 1907, House Miscellaneous Document No. 210, pts. 1-10, 10 vols (Washington, D.C.: Government Printing Office, 1907), 4,16.

B.   Richardson, J. D., ed. Compilation of the Messages and Papers of the Presidents, 1789-1897, 53rd Cong., 2nd sess., 1907, House Miscellaneous Document No. 210, pts. 1-10, 10 vols. Washington, D.C.: Government Printing Office, 1907.

N.   [12]United States, President, <u>Public Papers</u>
        <u>of the Presidents of the United States</u> (Wash-
        ington, D.C.: Office of the <u>Federal Register</u>,
        National Archives and Records Service, 1953-),
        Dwight D. Eisenhower, 1956, pp. 222-23.

B.   United States, President. <u>Public Papers of the</u>
        <u>Presidents of the United States</u>.
        Washington, D.C.: Office of the <u>Federal</u>
        <u>Register</u>, National Archives and Records
        Service, 1953- , Dwight D. Eisenhower, 1956.

9:21   After their passage, bills and joint and concurrent resolutions
are cited as statutes. Those that have gone into effect during
the year are published in the *Statutes at Large* (n. 13 below),
which since 1939 have been issued annually at the close of the
calendar year. Later, the statutes are published in the *United
States Code*. *Code* citation is preferred when it is available (n.
14). As a matter of convenience to the reader, a statute is
sometimes given a parallel citation to the *Statutes at Large* (n.
15):

N.   [13]<u>Administrative Procedure Act</u>, <u>Statutes at</u>
        <u>Large</u> 60, sec. 10, 243 (1946).

B.   <u>Administrative Procedure Act</u>. <u>Statutes at Large</u>,
        vol. 60 (1946).

N.   [14]<u>Declaratory Judgment Act</u>, <u>United States</u>
        <u>Code</u>, vol. 28, secs 2201-2 (1952). [Citations to
        the <u>Code</u> are always to section number, not page.]

B.   <u>Declaratory Judgment Act</u>, <u>United States Code</u>,
        vol. 28 (1952).

N.   [15]<u>Labor Management Relations Act</u> (Taft-
        Hartley Act), <u>Statutes at Large</u> 61, sec. 301(a),
        156 (1947). <u>United States Code</u>, vol. 39, sec. 185(a)
        (1952).

B.   <u>Labor Management Relations Act</u> (Taft-Hartley
        Act). <u>Statutes at Large</u>, vol. 61 (1947).
        <u>United States Code</u>, vol. 39 (1952).

9:22   The United States Constitution is referred to by article and
section (by clause as well, if relevant). If the reference is to an
amendment, that must be cited by number following
Constitution:

N.   [16]United States, <u>Constitution</u>, art. I, sec. 4

B.   United States. <u>Constitution</u>. Art. I, sec. 4.

N.   [17]United States, <u>Constitution</u>, amend. XIV, sec. 2.

B.   United States. <u>Constitution</u>. Amend. XIV, sec. 2.

9:23   The several government commissions, such as the Federal Communications Commission, Federal Trade Commission, Securities and Exchange Commission, also publish bulletins, circulars, reports, study papers, and the like. Often, those communications are classified as House or Senate Documents:

N.   [18]United States, Congress, Senate, <u>Report of the Federal Trade Commission on Utility Corporations</u>, S. Doc. 92, 70th Cong., 1st sess., 1935, pt 71A.

B.   United States. Congress. Senate. <u>Report of the Federal Trade Commission on Utility Corporations</u>. S. Doc. 92, 70th Cong., 1st sess., 1935.

EXECUTIVE DEPARTMENT DOCUMENTS

9:24   Executive department documents consist of reports of executive departments and bureaux, bulletins, circulars, and miscellaneous materials. Many departmental publications are classified in series, and some have personal authors whose names are given in the citations (n. 2 below). It is not desirable, however, to cite government publications by names of personal authors. Few libraries catalogue them except under the name of the sponsoring government agency. (J. D. Richardson, editor of the *Compilation of the Messages and Papers of the Presidents*, is a notable exception.)

N.   [1]United States, Department of Health, Education, and Welfare, <u>Proceedings, 1961 Conference of the Surgeon-General, Public Health Service, and Chief, Children's Bureau, with State and Territorial Health Officers, 8-10 August 1961</u>, pp. 8-10.

B.   United States. Department of Health, Education and
      Welfare. Proceedings, 1961 Conference of the
      Surgeon-General, Public Health Service, and
      Chief, Children's Bureau, with State and
      Territorial Health Officers, 8-10 August 1961.

N.   [2]United States, Department of Agriculture,
      Farm Security Administration and Bureau of
      Agricultural Economics Co-operating, Analysis of
      70,000 Rural Rehabilitation Farmlands, by
      E. L. Kirkpatrick, Social Research Report No. 9
      (Washington, D.C.: Government Printing Office,
      1938), pp. 19-32.

B.   United States. Department of Agriculture. Farm
      Security Administration and Bureau of
      Agricultural Economics Co-operating. Analysis
      of 70,000 Rural Rehabilitation Farmlands, by
      E. L. Kirkpatrick. Social Research Report No. 9.
      Washington, D.C.: Government Printing Office,
      1938.

N.   [3]United States, Department of State,
      Declaration of the U.N. Conference on Food and
      Agriculture, War Documents Series Pubn. No. 2162
      (1944), pp. 6-8.

B.   United States. Department of State. Declaration of
      the U.N. Conference on Food and Agriculture.
      War Documents Series Pubn. No. 2162 (1944).

N.   [4]United States, Department of State, Public
      Roads Program in the Philippines, Treaties and
      Other International Acts Series 1584, Pubn. 2805
      (1947), p. 3. [The number 1584 is the number of
      the "treaty" as assigned by the State Department.]

B.   United States. Department of State. Public Roads
      Program in the Philippines. Treaties and
      Other International Acts Series 1584, Pubn.
      2805 (1947).

N.   [5]United States, Department of Interior,
      Office of Indian Affairs, Annual Report of the
      Commissioner of Indian Affairs to the Secretary
      of the Interior, for the Fiscal Year Ended 30 June
      1932, p.24

B.   United States. Department of Interior. Office of
      Indian Affairs. Annual Report of the
      Commissioner of Indian Affairs to the
      Secretary of the Department of the Interior,
      for the Fiscal Year Ended 30 June 1932.

N.   [6]United States, Department of Commerce,
      Bureau of the Census, <u>Fifteenth Census of the
      United States, 1930: Population,</u> 2:98.

B.   United States. Department of Commerce. Bureau of
            the Census. <u>Fifteenth Census of the United
            States, 1930: Population,</u> vol. 2.

N.   [7]United States, Department of Commerce,
      Bureau of the Census, <u>United States Census of
      Population: 1960,</u> vol. 1, <u>Characteristics of the
      Population,</u> pt. 6, California.

B.   United States. Department of Commerce. Bureau of
            the Census. <u>United States Census of
            Population: 1960.</u> Vol. 1, <u>Characteristics of
            the Population,</u> pt. 6, California.

9:25   Since 1950, treaties have been published in the *United States
Treaties and Other International Agreements* (n. 8), the
annual bound volumes of the papers as they were numbered
and published by the Department of State in pamphlet form
in the series Treaties and Other International Acts (para.
9:24, n. 4). With the inauguration of the new series,
publication was discontinued in the *Statutes at Large*.
Multilateral treaties appear in the Treaty Series of the United
Nations (n. 10), although usually a year or more after their
signature. Treaties predating 1950 may be found (depending
upon their nature and date) in the Treaty Series of the League
of Nations, the Treaty Series and Executive Agreement Series
of the Department of State, and in the *Statutes at Large* (n.
9):

N.   [8]United States, Department of State, <u>United
      States Treaties and Other International Agreements,</u>
      vol. 14, pt. 2, "Nuclear Weapons Test Ban", TIAS
      No. 5433, 5 August 1963.

B.   United States. Department of State. <u>United States
            Treaties and Other International Agreements,</u>
            vol. 14, pt. 2. "Nuclear Weapons Test Ban",
            TIAS No. 5433, 5 August 1963.

N.   [9]United States, <u>Statutes at Large,</u> vol. 43,
      pt. 2 (December 1923--March 1925), "Naval Armament
      Limitation Treaty", 26 February 1922.

B.   United States. <u>Statutes at Large,</u> vol. 43, pt. 2
            (December 1923--March 1925). "Naval Armament
            Limitation Treaty", 26 February 1922.

N.   [10]United Nations, Treaty Series, <u>Treaties
and International Agreements Registered or Filed
and Reported with the Secretariat of the United
Nations</u>, vol. 250 (1956), No. 3516, "Denmark
and Italy: Convention concerning Military Service",
15 July 1954, p. 45.

B.   United Nations. Treaty Series. <u>Treaties and
International Agreements Registered or Filed
and Reported with the Secretariat of the
United Nations</u>, vol. 250 (1956), No. 3516,
"Denmark and Italy: Convention concerning
Military Service", 15 July 1954.

STATE AND LOCAL GOVERNMENT DOCUMENTS

9:26   Citations to state and local government documents are in
essentially the same form as those to United States
government documents:

N.   [1]Illinois, <u>Constitution</u> (1848), art. 5,
sec. 2. |Ordinarily, the date of a constitution is
indicated only when it is not in force.|

B.   Illinois. <u>Constitution</u> (1848).

N.   [2]Kentucky, <u>Revised Statutes, Annotated</u>
(Baldwin, 1943). |The style used in referring
to an annotated revision made by William E.
Baldwin in 1943.|

B.   Kentucky. <u>Revised Statutes, Annotated</u> (Baldwin,
1943).

N.   [3]Ohio, <u>Judicial Organization Act</u>, <u>Statutes</u>
(1830) 3:1671-78.

B.   Ohio. <u>Judicial Organization Act</u>. <u>Statutes</u> (1830),
vol. 3.

N.   [4]New York, N.Y., <u>"Good Samaritan" Law</u>,
<u>Administrative Code</u> (1965), sec. 67-3.2.

B.   New York, N.Y. <u>"Good Samaritan" Law</u>. <u>Adminis-
trative Code</u> (1965).

LEAGUE OF NATIONS AND UNITED NATIONS DOCUMENTS

9:27   For these documents, the authorizing body, the topic of the paper, the document number, and the date must be given in the references:

N.   [1]League of Nations, Secretariat, <u>Appli-cation of Part II of the Opium Convention</u> (O.C. 114) (1923), p. 5.

B.   League of Nations. Secretariat. <u>Application of Part II of the Opium Convention</u> (O.C. 114) (1923).

N.   [2]United Nations, Economic and Social Council, Social Commission, 17th Session, <u>Reappropriation of the Role of the Social Commission: Report of the Secretary-General</u> (E/CN. 5/400), 16 February 1966, pp. 9-10.

B.   United Nations. Economic and Social Council, Social Commission, 17th Session. <u>Reappro-priation of the Role of the Social Commission: Report of the Secretary-General</u> (E/CN. 5/400), 16 February 1966.

N.   [3]United Nations, General Assembly, 17th Session, 8 October 1966, <u>Report of the Special Committee on the Situation with Regard to the Implementation of the Declaration on the Granting of Independence to Colonial Countries and Peoples</u> (A/5238), annex 1, p. 3.

B.   United Nations. General Assembly, 17th Session, 8 October 1966. <u>Report of the Special Committee on the Situation with Regard to the Implementation of the Declaration on the Granting of Independence to Colonial Countries and Peoples</u> (A/5238).

N.   [4]United Nations, World Health Organiza-tion, <u>Toxic Hazards of Pesticides to Man: Twelfth Report of the Expert Committee on Insecticides</u> (WHO Technical Report Series, no. 227), 1962, pp. 6-10.

B.   United Nations. World Health Organization. <u>Toxic Hazards of Pesticides to Man: Twelfth Report of the Expert Committee on Insecticides</u>. WHO Technical Report Series, no. 227, 1962.

10   Tables

10:1   If tables are satisfactorily to serve the purpose for which they are made, not only must they be accurately compiled but they must be so arranged that they can be easily read and interpreted. To these ends careful spacing, ruling, arrangement of headings, and, finally, the placing of the tables with respect to the text all contribute.

NUMBERING

10:2   In general every table should be given a number and a title, even though there may be few tables in the paper. (A very simple tabulation introduced in such a way that a caption seems unnecessary should not be given a number.) The order in which the tables are mentioned in the text determines the numbering.

10:3   Tables in an appendix should be numbered consecutively with the tables in the text. That is, if the last table in the text is table 52, the first table in the appendix is table 53.

POSITION

10:4   Numbering tables aids the typist in placing them. All text references to a table should be by number, for example, "As table 3 shows . . ." or "(see table 3)", never by an introductory phrase such as "in the following table". With all references by number and no colon demanding immediate inclusion of the table, the text may be typed to the end of the page or the paragraph and the table inserted where its size permits.

10:5   Ideally, each table should be placed as close to the first reference to it as possible. If space permits, however, it is best to finish the paragraph of text in which the reference occurs before inserting the table. If a table cannot be accommodated in the remaining space available for it on a given page, it should be placed on the next page, either (if it is long enough) by itself or else with text following it. If a table is just a few lines too long for a page, it may be shortened by using one-and-one-half-line spacing instead of double spacing.

10:6   In typing tables with text, three spaces should be left above and three spaces below each table (i.e., the table number is typed on the third space following the text, and the text is continued on the third space below the bottom rule).

S I Z E

10:7   Most tables may be typed so that columns run the long way on the page. A table may occupy the full width of the typed page or, if the number and width of columns permit, less than the full width. In either case each table must be centred horizontally upon the page (see table 1).

LONG AND NARROW

10:8   When a table is long and narrow, space may be saved by doubling up—dividing it in equal parts and placing them side by side (see table 2). Note the vertical double line separating the two parts.

WIDE

10:9   If a table is too wide for the page, it should be turned lengthwise—that is, the paper is put in the typewriter sideways and the table is typed so that the columns run the short way of the paper. Table number and title are at the binding side of the page. A table so typed is called a *landscape* table (see table 6). No text should be typed on a page containing a landscape table.

10:10   If too wide to be accommodated landscape, a table may be arranged on two facing pages (see table 7). This is done physically by turning the first page over so that the typed side is on the back and thus faces the next page (the other side of the first page, now the front, remains blank).[1] The parts of the table must be of the same dimensions on both pages, and special care in typing will be required to ensure that the appropriate figure in each column is exactly in line with the item in the stub (i.e., first column) to which it belongs.

10:11   Tables too wide to be accommodated on the 210 × 297 mm. (A4) page in either of the ways described may be typed on two or more pages, which then may be pasted together and reduced to page size by a suitable photographic process; or, less satisfactorily for the use of any paper that is to be bound and placed in a library, a large table may be folded. (See paras. 11:29–31.)

CONTINUING LONG

10:12   Long tables may be continued from page to page. The table number and the caption are typed at the beginning of the table; the table number only on succeeding pages, written, for example, "TABLE   2—*Continued.*"   Ordinarily,   the boxheadings above the columns are repeated on every page, except that, in a continued landscape table in which the pages face each other, the headings need not be repeated on the second page (and the fourth, sixth, etc.). In a table that is continued, the bottom rule is omitted except on the last page, at the end of the table.

CAPTIONS

10:13   It is necessary to give each numbered table a title, or caption. If a very brief tabulation is introduced in such a way that a caption seems unnecessary, the tabulation should not be given a table number.

10:14   In typing the table number and caption, centre "TABLE 00" all in capital letters on a line by itself, with the number in arabic numerals. Centre the caption, also in capital letters, on

---

[1]If the paper is to be bound, a note to the binder, in addition to the correct placement of the pages, will ensure accurate results.

the second space below the table number. If the caption is longer than the width of the table, set it in two or more lines, arranged in inverted pyramid form and single-spaced. If table captions contain chemical, physical, or mathematical expressions conventionally expressed in small letters, rather than capitals, these expressions should be so typed, even though the rest of the caption is in capitals (see also para. 10:15).

10:15   If the captions of most of the tables are two or more lines in length, time and space would be saved by using a different style of caption from that just described. Type the table number as just directed, but place it at the edge of the table rather than in the centre; add a full stop and a dash, and continue with the caption, typing the first and all succeeding full lines the full width of the table and centring the last, shorter line. Capitalization may either follow the rules for capitalizing titles of works (para. 4:6) or the system where only the first word and all proper nouns and proper adjectives are capitalized:

```
TABLE 21.--Probable rate of damage per foot-
candle for thirty light sources expressed in
        percentage relative to zenith day
```

Type all captions in a consistent style throughout the paper.

BOXHEADINGS

10:16   Column headings, called boxheadings, may be of one level or of two or more levels. The first level, spanner headings, are set off by rules and centred above the subsumed headings below (see table 5). Centre each heading above the column it identifies, leaving the same amount of blank space above and below the headings. Never place a horizontal rule immediately beneath a heading lest the rule be mistaken for underlining of the words. To allow for the vertical rules, leave at least one space at either end of the longest line of each heading.

10:17   Boxheadings may be typed vertically if necessary to save space. They should be set so as to read up from the bottom of the page (see table 6). Where turnover lines are unavoidable in a boxheading, they should be typed single space.

10:18 It is a convenience for the columns to be numbered when the textual discussion refers to individual columns. The numbers should be enclosed in parentheses and centred on the first line below the boxheadings. The stub column is not numbered (See table 3.)

CUT-IN HEADINGS

10:19 To avoid an excessive number of levels of boxheadings (three at the outside), it is sometimes possible to insert a head that cuts across the body of the table and applies to the tabular matter lying below it (see table 5). Cut-in heads should be centred and capitalized in the same style as the boxheadings.

CAPITALIZATION

10:20 Adapt the capitalization of the boxheadings to that of the caption according to the following scheme: if the caption either is in capitals throughout or is capitalized as a title of a work (see para. 4:6), the boxheadings should be capitalized as titles. But if the caption employs capitals only for first word, proper nouns, and proper adjectives (see para. 10:15), the capitalization of the boxheadings should agree.

STUB

10:21 The left-hand column of a table, known as the stub, has no boxheading unless one is necessary for identification. Only the first word and proper names are capitalized. If the individual items require runover lines, they are indented to the third space. When an item is subdivided, however, the subdivisions are indented three spaces and any runovers are indented further:

```
Coastal district vs. interior
   district . . . . . . . . .
```

```
But:
Relative to issue
      price:
    1923-27 . . . .
    1949-55 . . . .
```

Another way to show subdivision in a stub is to underline the main entry but not the subdivisions, aligning all at the left (table 4).

10:22   If a *Total, Mean* or *Average* appears in the stub, the word should be indented. If both *Total* and *Grand total* are given, the latter is indented further (see para. 10:40).

10:23   If the open space between the end of a line in the stub and the columnar matter to which it refers is such that the eye does not move easily from one to the other, leaders (spaced periods) should connect the two (see table 4). If one table in a paper requires leaders, all should have them.

OMISSIONS

10:24   In a long column of figures, zero preceding a decimal point may be omitted from all entries except the first and the last. Degree, pound and dollar signs ($°,£,\$$) must appear at the top of each column, where relevant, and after every break in a column, such as rules above totals and cut-in headings.

10:25   If all the figures in a table are in thousands or millions, space may be saved by omitting the relevant zeros and noting the fact at the end of the caption, as, for example, "(Figures in millions)". (See table 4.)

10:26   A blank space in a column should be indicated by spaced leaders, which should be at least three in number and centred with respect to the longest number in the column (see table 7) or the number necessary to occupy the full width of the column. Use one or other of these styles consistently.

ALIGNMENT

10:27   The items in the stub should be aligned with their related items in the columns. If the stub item occupies more than one line and the column entry one, align on the last line of the stub; if both contain more than one line, align on the first line and omit leaders:

```
Mean water content
    (per cent) . . . . . 69.6
```

But:
```
C₂(35"-50"+) (fresh      Dark greyish brown
    till, slightly          (10 YR 4/2) boul-
    oxidized)               dery loamy sand;
                            massive structure;
                            pH of 6.42
```

10:28 Vertically, in a column of figures align all decimal points and commas. Note that every figure of 1,000 or more must have a comma (see para. 2:51). Align also pound and dollar signs and plus, minus, plus-minus, and equals signs. When the number of digits varies, allow for the longest number.

ABBREVIATIONS AND SYMBOLS

10:29 Although prohibited for the most part in text, abbreviations and symbols are legitimate space-savers in box- and cut-in headings and in the main body of tables, but not in captions (except mathematical and chemical symbols). Standard abbreviations should be used if they exist; if they do not, the writer may devise his own, explaining them in a note or key unless they are self-explanatory. Abbreviations must be consistent for all tables.

10:30 Symbols that cannot be made with the typewriter should be inserted by hand, using permanent black ink (indian ink preferred).

FOOTNOTES TO TABLES

10:31 Footnotes to tables may be of three kinds: source notes, general notes, and notes referring to specific parts of the table. The term "source note" is self-explanatory: if a writer has not compiled the data for a table himself, he must identify his source. General notes might include remarks on the reliability of the data presented or of the way they were collected or handled; such notes apply to the entire table. These two kinds of notes do not require reference symbols in the table; they are introduced, respectively, by the words SOURCE(S) and NOTE(S).

10:32   Notes to specific parts of a table require reference symbols. If the table consists of information in words only, superior numerals may be used as reference indexes. If the table consists wholly or partly of figures, either superior letters ([a,b]) or symbols (*,**) should be used. If it includes mathematical or chemical formulas requiring notes, symbols rather than superior letters or figures must be employed.

10:33   Footnotes to tables must not be numbered in the same series as text notes. A new series of reference numbers, or symbols, is begun for each table.

10:34   The notes should appear in the following order: source notes, general notes, and notes to specific parts; and they should be placed immediately below the table, not at the foot of the page below lines of text. Begin the first note on the second space below the bottom rule of the table. Each note should have a paragraph indention and the notes should be typed to the full width of the table, except under double-page tables. Single-space runover lines, but double-space between notes.

10:35   If a table employing symbols as reference marks requires no more than three, double and triple asterisks may be used, but if more than three are required, additional symbols must be used: † (dagger), ‡ (double dagger), # (number sign). The use of more than three asterisks or of a combination of asterisks and superior letters is not permissible. The same scheme of reference marks should be used for all tables.

RULING

10:36   Since some institutions specify that all tables be ruled and others allow considerable latitude, it is advisable for the student to discuss the matter with the appropriate staff member. The following suggestions are for those who must make their own decisions.

TABLE 1
MULTIPLE CORRELATION COEFFICIENTS
OF PROBABILITY FUNCTIONS

Range of Values	No. Observed Values
0-.199	15
.2-.399	1
.4-.599	1

TABLE 2
CASES FILED, TERMINATED, AND PENDING IN THE COURT OF APPEALS
FOR THE THIRD CIRCUIT, FISCAL YEARS 1940-1949, INCLUSIVE

Fiscal Year	Com-menced	Termi-nated	Pend-ing	Fiscal Year	Com-menced	Termi-nated	Pend-ing
1940 . . .	322	360	170	1945	299	268	226
1941 . . .	285	350	102	1946	197	274	149
1942 . . .	292	222	172	1947	266	216	199
1943 . . .	353	302	223	1948	287	250	236
1944 . . .	276	304	195	1949 (1st half)	128	113	251

TABLE 3
OLDER WORKERS IN FRANCE BY OCCUPATION, 1956

Occupation	Men Aged 65 and over (in thousands) (1)	Men Percentage following principal occupation (2)	Women Aged 65 and over (in thousands) (3)	Women Percentage following principal occupation (4)
Farm owners	508	42	652	14
Farm labourers	140	20	124	3
Owners of business and industry	302	40	352	26
Professional workers and managers of business and industry . .	202	21	82	7
Clerical workers	148	12	122	3
Manual workers	482	18	376	13
Artists, clergy, army, police .	70	17	4	50
Domestic service	50	32	366	16
Never employed	18	. . . . . .	948	. . . . . .
Total	1,920	28	3,026	10

TABLE 4
ESTIMATED NATIONAL INCOME OF INDIA, AT 1948-49 PRICES
1900-1901 TO 1950-51, BY SELECTED YEARS
(Money Amounts in Millions of Rupees)

	1900-1901	1910-11	1920-21	1930-31	1940-41	1950-51
Total income						
Amount	51,090	62,410	64,690	76,840	86,460	91,920
Index	100.0	122.1	126.6	150.4	169.2	179.9
Agricultural production						
Amount	39,760	44,330	38,070	45,980	45,340	44,050
Index	100.0	111.5	95.7	115.6	114.0	110.8
All other industries						
Amount	11,330	18,080	26,620	30,860	41,120	48,070
Index	100.0	159.6	234.9	272.4	362.9	424.8

SOURCE: V. K. R. V. Rao, A. K. Ghosh, M.V. Divatia, and Um Datta, eds., Papers on National Income and Allied Topics, Indian Conference on Research in National Income 2 (Bombay: Asia Publishing House, 1962):22-23, table 3.

TABLE 5
EFFECT OF A SINGLE 24-HOUR EXPOSURE TO 33 DEGREES C. DURING
DIFFERENT PERIODS OF PUPAL DEVELOPMENT
REMAINDER OF TIME AT 25 DEGREES C.

Period at 33 Degrees	No. Flies Emerged	Time in Days			Percentage of Development					
		Low Temp.	High Temp.	Total	Per Day		Low Temp.	High Temp.	Total	Total -100
					Low Temp.	High Temp.				
Males										
First day	61	3.31	1.00	4.31±0.009	23.47	27.54	77.68	27.54	105.22	+5.22
Second day	64	3.27	1.00	4.27±0.009	23.47	27.54	76.74	27.54	104.28	+4.28
Third day	62	3.14	1.00	4.14±0.020	23.47	27.54	73.69	27.54	101.23	+1.23
Fourth day	66	3.00	0.92	3.92+0.005	23.47	27.54	70.41	25.33	95.74	-4.26
Females										
First day	39	3.08	1.00	4.08±0.009	24.87	28.57	76.59	28.57	105.16	+5.16
Second day	53	2.94	1.00	3.94±0.006	24.87	28.57	73.11	28.57	101.68	+1.68
Third day	58	2.82	1.00	3.82±0.011	24.87	28.57	70.13	28.57	98.70	-1.30
Fourth day	51	3.00	0.86	3.66±0.007	24.87	28.57	74.64	24.57	99.21	-0.79

TABLE 6

VALUE ADDED BY MANUFACTURER PER PRODUCTION WORKER (IN DOLLARS), SOUTH BEND STANDARD METROPOLITAN AREA AND SEVEN SELECTED STANDARD METROPOLITAN AREAS, 1947

Census Groups and Code Number	South Bend	South Bend Rank among Selected Standard Metropolitan Areas	Chicago	Indianapolis	St. Louis	Detroit	Toledo	Grand Rapids	Milwaukee
20. Food & kindred products . .	9,183	5	9,340	8,585	8,777	8,296	7,600	7,709	11,932
23. Apparel & related products .	3,797	11	5,397	5,017	4,588	5,170	4,495	5,081	4,732
24. Lumber & products, except furniture	5,629	2	5,503	3,700	4,464	7,569	5,124	–	5,262
26. Paper & allied products . .	7,111	6	6,605	7,286	5,781	6,491	6,629	5,168	7,804
27. Printing & publishing industries	9,767	4	9,125	10,040	8,660	11,528	10,350	7,858	7,888
32. Stone, clay & glass products	4,033	11	6,558	6,058	5,663	6,563	10,284	8,990	6,383
33. Primary metal industries . .	6,397	4	6,689	4,321	5,599	5,600	6,668	6,049	6,453
34. Fabricated metal products . .	5,351	10	6,534	5,037	5,687	5,569	5,759	5,263	6,928
35. Machinery, except electrical.	6,048	10	6,656	5,502	5,756	6,847	7,298	5,884	6,368
36. Electrical machinery.	6,613	6	6,682	6,614	6,054	6,862	5,823	7,022 [a]	6,243
39. Miscellaneous manufactures. .	4,755	7	6,042	5,521	4,760	5,825	4,608	. . .[a]	4,642

SOURCE: U.S. Department of Commerce, Bureau of the Census, Census of Manufactures: 1947, vol. 3, Statistics by States (Washington, D.C.: Government Printing Office, 1948), pp. 205-9, 308-18, 343-50, 479-81, 483, 648-49.

[a]Complete figures are not provided by the Census.

TABLE 7
CASE LOAD PER JUDGESHIP FOR THE NORTHERN DISTRICT OF FLORIDA
FOR THE FISCAL YEARS 1940-48, INCLUSIVE
(CASES FILED PER JUDGE)

Fiscal Year	Number of Judges, Florida (Northern)	Total Civil Cases per Judge		Criminal Cases per Judge	
		Florida (Northern)	84 Districts	Florida (Northern)	84 Districts
1940	1	95	153	191	178
1941	1	104	164	247	165
1942	1	103	168	147	174
1943	1	79	158	105	190
1944	1	70	169	161	211
1945	1	98	295	239	209
1946	1	131	321	125	171
1947	1	106	271	110	173
1948	1	85	205	206	167

10:37 Two-column tables are best left without any rules (see table 1). In general, all tables of more than two columns should carry vertical rules throughout. It is permissible, however, to omit the rules between columns covered by a spanner heading (see para. 10:16), provided that the columns are not too close together. In table 3 omission of a rule between columns 1 and 2 and between columns 3 and 4 is allowable; but in table 5 the columns of figures are so close together that rules are important for ease of reading, and therefore are not omitted. It is increasingly common to omit all vertical rules, even in very large tables, and this is permissible if columns are appropriately spaced. Such tables are termed "open-style" (see table 6).

10:38 Each ruled table should have a double rule at the top, above the boxheading, and a single rule at the bottom, or end, of the table. There are no vertical rules at the sides of the table.

TABLE 7-<u>Continued</u>

Florida (North-ern)	84 Districts	Florida (North-ern)	84 Districts	Florida (North-ern)	84 Districts	Florida (North-ern)	84 Districts
61	72	...	...	61	72	34	81
59	83	...	...	59	83	45	82
70	91	...	...	70	91	33	77
49	100	...	12	49	88	30	58
47	113	7	37	40	76	23	56
70	238	6	160	64	78	28	57
03	251	71	174	32	77	28	70
80	162	30	84	50	78	26	109
63	87	6	20	57	67	22	117

Column groups: United States Civil Cases per Judge (United States a Party) — Total, OPA, Other United States; and Private Civil Cases per Judge, Total.

10:39 It has been noted that blank space should be left on all sides of a boxheading (see para. 10:16). Never begin a heading on the line immediately below the rule, and never begin a rule on the same line as a heading (thus giving the effect of underlined words).

10:40 A rule should be typed above totals at the feet of columns, across the columns but not extending through the stub (see table 3). Subtotals, grand totals, means, and averages are similarly handled.

10:41 Horizontal rules are usually made with the typewriter; vertical rules by hand (using permanent black ink, preferably indian ink). A double rule is typed by turning the knob of the roller just slightly before typing the second line. If the carriage of the typewriter takes the paper the long way, all the rules may be made with the typewriter. But using the typewriter to make the vertical rules requires special care if the columns are only one or two spaces apart.

11   Illustrations

11:1   In addition to tables, illustrative materials may consist of graphs (pies, curves, and map graphs), charts showing organization of departments, plans, and so on, diagrams of machines and instruments, maps, photographs, commercial illustrations, and original illustrations. Such illustrations are also called "figures".

11:2   It is not within the scope of this *Manual* to give advice on the inclusion of illustrative materials, or on what type or types to use, or, except in general terms, to give instructions on their presentation. However, some general principles need to be summarized to bring the preparation of illustrative materials for a paper into harmony with that of the text.

POSITION

11:3   Illustrations, especially graphs and charts, should be placed as close as possible to their first references in the text. Like tables, they should be referred to by number so that their exact placement is flexible (see para. 10:4). In some papers there may be sound reasons for grouping all the illustrations, if they are of one type, at the end. (In a printed book, photographs and other illustrations printed on paper different from that of the text are frequently placed together rather than scattered through the text.)

PAGE NUMBERS

11:4   When illustrative materials are included with the text, their pages are numbered consecutively with the textual matter. It is not permissible to give them supplementary numbers (e.g.,

45*a*) after the text has been numbered. A folded map or chart is numbered in the centre at the top of the exposed fold. A frontispiece, which faces the title page, is numbered with the preliminaries, but the page number does not appear.

11:5   Pages of illustrations placed together at the end of the paper should follow the pagination of the text.

MARGINS

11:6   A margin of at least one inch (more is permissible) should be allowed on all four sides of a page carrying illustrative material. The number of the illustration and its caption or legend (everything but the number of the page) must fall within the margins (for margins when mounting material, see para. 11:25).

NUMBERS AND LEGENDS

11:7   If a paper contains several types of illustrations such as maps, charts, diagrams, and graphs, it is desirable to label them all as figures and number them consecutively, in arabic numerals. If, however, there is a disproportionately large number of one type, or one type which, though not greater in number than the others, is seen to be of greater importance for the study, that type should be given its own label and numbered in a separate series: Map 1 or Chart 3 or Graph 4. (See sample F, p. 14.)

11:8   Ordinarily a legend follows the number; this may be in the form of a title, or caption:

Fig. 2   Block diagram of Fern Lake

But it is frequently in the form of an explanation consisting of a sentence or more (not necessarily grammatically complete sentences) of explanation. Here the first line is indented like a paragraph and the punctuation follows ordinary sentence style:

Fig. 9.   Relationship between number of buds or leaf scars, number of branches subsequently produced, and length of shoots. Small numbers identify multiple observations of same value.

181

11:9   The legend should be typed to the width of the illustration, except that short legends are centred.

11:10   Two or more illustrations may appear on the same page, each with its number and legend. Also, two or more related illustrations may be placed on the same page, the group as a whole being given a number and a legend, and the individual illustrations being identified by letter alone (a, b, etc.) or by letter and legend. If space below the individual illustrations is not sufficient for both the letter and the legend, each illustration may simply be lettered, and letters and legends either be grouped at the foot of the page or typed on the opposite page. In the latter instance, the page with the legend is turned over so that the reader will see illustration and legend on facing pages (see para. 10:10).

11:11   A wide illustration may be placed landscape on the page, with the top at the binding side. The legend, with its number, should appear below the illustration, so that it reads up the page. The page number is in its normal position. This same arrangement may be used for a group of illustrations.

11:12   Some illustrations, maps in particular, carry printed or hand-lettered headings at the top or the side of the illustration. In such a case only the number of the illustration is centred below it.

11:13   A key, or scale of miles, if included, should preferably be placed in a convenient space beside the illustration rather than below it.

11:14   If the space below an illustration is not sufficient to carry the number and legend and still allow the one-inch margin at the bottom of the page, they may be centred at the right of the illustration. If there is not enough space at the side, number and legend may be typed on the opposite page (see para. 11:10).

PREPARATION

GRAPHS AND CHARTS

11:15   Line graphs and bar charts may be either (1) drawn in indian ink on cross-ruled paper of the same, or approximately the same, quality as the paper used for the text; (2) drawn first on cross-ruled paper, traced on the plain bond paper, and the lines inked in; or (3) drawn first and then reproduced by a suitable photographic process. Graph paper is available ruled either in the metric system or in inches and fractions thereof. Also, the paper is made with lines in one of several colours: black, brown, red, green, violet, blue. The choice of colour may depend upon whether the drawing is to be photographed and whether it is desired to show the entire grid system. The pale blue lines will not reproduce in the photographic process.

11:16   When fine detail is to be shown in an illustration, it is sometimes advisable, if not necessary, to make the original drawing larger than could be accommodated on 210 × 297 mm. (A4) paper. Made to scale, the illustration is then reduced to page size by photography.

PHOTOGRAPHS

11:17   Photographs may be finished either in the 210 × 297 mm. (A4) size so as to avoid mounting, or smaller and mounted two or more to a page on the regular typing paper. If photographs are finished full size, the paper should be medium weight, since the heavier weight tends to break in binding. Matt surface photographs may be preferred to glossy prints, although the latter make sharper illustrations and are therefore a better choice where minute detail must be shown.

11:18   Commercial illustrations usually require mounting. If several copies of these are needed, and are not available, the originals may be reproduced photographically. If the illustrations are in colour, however, photographs may not be satisfactory. The inclusion of illustrations in colour requires considerable forethought. As a matter of fact, colour cannot be used in a thesis or dissertation for a university or college which requires a planographic or microphotographic reproduction of its theses and dissertations. The photographs and photographic reproductions for use in such theses or dissertations should be on glossy paper.

MAPS

11:19   Many kinds of maps are available ready-made, and some may serve satisfactorily with no additions except page and figure number and, possibly, a caption. Some may be used as base maps, with crosshatching, outlining of specific areas, spotting, figures or letters superimposed to produce illustrations adequate for the writer's particular purposes. Unless stippling or crosshatching of only a small area is required, handwork should not be attempted. A number of commercial products offer satisfactory methods in combination with handwork. Where stippling or crosshatching is required, the products of such firms as Zipatone, Letraset, Mecanorma or Magictype may be employed. These are all available in the United Kingdom and may be obtained in either self-adhesive or dry transfer forms.

11:20   Maps often need to be executed entirely by hand. In the fields of geography and geology, where knowledge of maps and map-making is so important an objective in the student's training, hand-made maps in theses and dissertations, at least, are likely to be a requirement.

HANDWORK

11:21   Legends and keys, as well as any necessary lines, letters, or symbols in the illustrations proper, may be made either with the typewriter or by hand, using black waterproof drawing ink. For hand lettering, the aid of a stencil or a lettering device such as Letraset is recommended to assure clear, even, well-spaced lettering. Since the use of colour is not always feasible, various styles of lines must be used in graphs employing two or more curves; and crosshatching, shading with dots and small circles, or similar devices should be used in bar charts. (See para. 11:19.)

MOUNTING

11:22   Illustrations measuring less than 210 × 297 mm. must be mounted on bond typing paper. Dry mounting tissue is the most satisfactory adhesive for the purpose. Properly applied (and correct application is most important) the mounts will remain firm for many years without causing the slightest deterioration of the illustrations. The tissue is available in sheets or in rolls, accompanied by complete directions for its use, and can be purchased from any photographic materials supplier.

11:23 Although dry mounting tissue is the preferred adhesive for mountings designed to withstand use for many years, some kinds of white casein glue are a reasonably satisfactory substitute, provided that the glue is applied in such a way that buckling does not result. The secret is in using a small enough quantity so that the liquid does not penetrate the body of the typing paper and cause it to stretch and wrinkle. It would be well to experiment before doing the final mountings. For small mounts, apply the glue thinly just within the edges of the mount. In addition, for larger pieces to be mounted, small dabs of glue applied here and there over the surface may be more satisfactory than its application at the edges alone. The adhesive is applied to the material that is to be mounted, not to the paper beneath it.

11:24 The use of rubber cement for mountings is discouraged.

11:25 Whether the adhesive used is dry mounting tissue or white casein glue, the area of the paper to be covered by the illustration should be indicated before the mounts are placed by drawing a very light pencil line at the top, or placing a dot at each upper corner. The illustration, or the composite of illustrations, should be centred upon the page. "Centring" in this connection assumes a slightly wider margin at the bottom of the sheet than at the top, and a half-inch wider margin at the left than at the right (to compensate for the visual loss due to the binding).

11:26 As each page of mounted material is finished, it should be set aside to dry for a few minutes (follow precisely the directions for drying mountings made with dry mounting tissue) before being placed under a weight for several hours. It is advisable to protect the newly mounted material by putting a piece of plain paper between each two sheets while they are under a weight.

11:27 A word of caution is not out of place to the student who proposes to develop and print his own photographs. The job should not be attempted by an amateur unless all the proper facilities are at hand and, further, unless there is ample time to carry out the successive steps without hurry and to allow for possible accidents.

11:28   It cannot be emphasized too strongly that sufficient time should be set aside for this job of mounting illustrations. Unless he is cautioned beforehand, the inexperienced person is likely to underestimate grossly the time that is required to do this work satisfactorily.

FOLDING

11:29   Illustrations larger than the normal page size may usually be reduced photographically. If reduction is not feasible, as it may not be in the case of large maps, for example, the material may be folded, provided that the institution for which the paper is prepared does not prohibit folding.

11:30   To fold, work first from right to left, making the first crease no more than 7½ inches from the left side of the sheet. If a second fold is necessary, carry the right-hand portion of the sheet back to the right, making the second crease no more than 6½ inches to the left of the first. Additional folds, if required, should be parallel with the first two. If the folding is done as directed, when the large folded sheet is in place, there will be no danger of the folds at the left being caught in the stitching or of those at the right being sheared off in the process of trimming.

11:31   Folding in more than one direction should be avoided, but, if it is not possible to do so, the sheet should first be folded from bottom to top, making the first fold no more than 10 inches from the top of the sheet. When this fold has been made, unfold the sheet and cut a strip 1 inch wide from the left-hand side of the sheet, starting at the bottom and continuing up to the fold. The removal of this strip is necessary to prevent the free portion of the sheet from being caught in the stitching. The sheet may then be refolded and folded from right to left as directed above.

12 Scientific Papers

12:1 It is difficult to generalize about the format of scientific papers as distinct from other kinds of scholarly papers, not only because even within the same field variable factors determine style to some extent.

A useful guide to follow is the current edition of The Royal Society, *General Notes on the Preparation of Scientific Papers*. It may also be necessary to consult the guide to authors issued by a specific periodical, such as *Nature*.

In general there are three major differences between format in non-scientific and in scientific papers: (1) organization, (2) handling of references, and (3) use of numerals, symbols, and abbreviations.

12:2 In such mechanical matters as spacing and pagination, and the presentation of tables and other illustrative materials, the scientific paper should conform in general to the style recommended in this *Manual* under the several headings.

ORGANIZATION

12:3 The length of a paper in part governs how it is divided into sections and whether the sections begin on new pages or not. In a short paper the sections do not usually begin on new pages; the text is typed continuously, with subheadings marking the sections. In longer papers the major sections may or may not be designated as chapters or parts, but usually each begins on a new page.

12:4 In shorter papers the major divisions may or may not be both numbered and titled, but they should be marked by either number or title. In all papers, subheadings usually appear within major divisions, but, in general, these should not begin new pages. (Suitable styles of subheadings and some suggestions on their logical order are discussed in para. 1:18.)

12:5   In short papers it is not necessary to include a table of contents, a list of tables, or a list of illustrations, although individual preferences or the demands of a specific piece of writing may call for one or all of these.

LIST OF REFERENCES

12:6   In papers in scientific fields, the general practice is to collect all the references at the end of the paper under some such headings as "List of References" or "Literature Cited". The term "Bibliography" appears less often, since for the most part it is not appropriate, the "List" usually being confined to those works mentioned in the paper. But if the list actually is a bibliography, it should be so headed.

12:7   Under the list scheme, regardless of its heading, footnotes are usually *not* employed to give sources. Instead, short references to items in the list appear in the text itself. There are two commonly used styles for this (see paras. 12:8, 12:12), the first of which is usually preferred.

12:8   Under the first scheme the text reference gives, in parentheses, the surname of the author with year date of the publication; or year date alone if the author's name occurs in the sentence:

These results were later confirmed (Naismith 1971).

Naismith (1971) was able to confirm these results.

12:9   The list of references at the end of the paper is arranged alphabetically by authors' surnames. Two or more works by the same author are listed chronologically, by date of publication. Two or more works by the same author published in the same year are identified as, for example, 1964*a*, 1964*b*. In a succession of works by the same author, the name is given for the first entry, and an eight-space line (i.e., the underlining key struck eight times) ending with a full stop replaces it in succeeding entries (see para. 7:24). If a title edited by the author follows immediately one of which he is the author, an eight-space line ending with a comma and followed by "ed." is used, but if the name is followed by a title of which he is co-author, his name should be repeated in full, followed by the names of his co-authors (see para. 7:9). Unless a particular purpose is served by numbering the entries in the list, numbering is omitted. Suggested styles of entries are the following:

Article

```
Mohr, H. 1962. Primary effect of light on growth.
     Ann. Rev. Plant Physiol. 13,465-88. |Note
     that capitalization of the title of the article
     should be that used in a sentence.|
```

Book

```
Kramer, P. J., and Kozlowski, T. T. 1960. Physiology
     of trees, p. 11. New York: McGraw-Hill.
     |"Sentence" capitalization for book title.|
```

12:10 If reference to a specific part of a work (such as a page, table or illustration) is desired, the notation should be included in the textual reference rather than in the entry in the list:

```
Analysis of the paired-data variance (Goulden 1952,
table 2) yields . . .
```

```
Ulrich (1927, p. 29 and fig. 2) divided the pairs . . .
```

12:11 In the examples of entries in a list of references (see para. 12:9), the reference to a journal article cites the title of the article, using capitalization as in a sentence. In some fields it is usual to omit the title of the article. The decision to include or to omit the titles must be made before the list is compiled, and one scheme followed consistently. The student may be guided in this decision by observing the general practice of journals in his field. If the paper is to be submitted to a specific journal for publication, it is well to follow exactly the style of reference used by that journal.

12:12 The second style of reference places a number after the author's name in the text, enclosing the number either in parentheses or in square brackets []:

> Whitehead [5] spoke of "nature alive" and "nature lifeless" . . .
>
> Numerous studies (21-35) have been published in which . . .

12:13   The items in the list are then numbered in sequence according to the first mention of each in the text. Subsequent references to a work use the same number. This scheme has the obvious disadvantage that it cannot be in alphabetical order and that no additional reference may be inserted in the text without renumbering all following items in the list; use of numbers such as 4*a* is not permitted. The scheme of reference described in paragraph 12:8, which is far less susceptible to error than that of paragraph 12:12, is therefore to be preferred.

12:14   Under either scheme, standard abbreviations for the names of journals are recommended. The writer should consult a list of abbreviations commonly used in his particular field. It is common practice to follow the current edition of the *World List of Scientific Periodicals* (Butterworth). There is also a British Standard (BS 4148) concerned with abbreviation of periodical titles.

If the names of publishers of books are given in shortened form, as is recommended, standard abbreviations should be used in accordance with the list given in *Books in Print*, published annually by R. R. Bowker Co., New York, or, for British publishers, in *British Books in Print: The Reference Catalogue of Current Literature*, published by J. Whitaker & Sons, London.

FOOTNOTES

12:15   Although the practice of collecting references in a list at the end of the paper appears to be growing in use, it is by no means uniform even within a given field, and the use of footnotes for citing references is not uncommon. The style of footnote entry used in chemistry is shown in paragraph 12:20; that in physics, in paragraph 12:22. If you do not know the style to use in your paper, you should consult the particular style manuals or guides prepared by the outstanding periodicals and associations in your field.

12:16 Relevant material not of sufficient importance to be brought into the text of the paper should be provided in a footnote. When the scheme adopted is to put references to the literature into footnotes, content footnotes should be numbered consecutively with the reference footnotes. When, however, the scheme is to put references to the literature into a list at the end of the paper, relevant remarks should not be incorporated into that list, but set as footnotes marked by an asterisk (*). If there is more than one note on a page, the second is marked by double asterisks (**), the third by triple asterisks (***). (See para. 10:35 for additional symbols. Do not use more than three asterisks.)

STYLES OF REFERENCE

12:17 The following examples are for entries in a list of references in some cases and for footnotes in others. They are patterned after the styles used by the leading publications in the several fields.

ANTHROPOLOGY

12:18 There is some variation in practice within this field. The scheme applied in *Man*, the periodical of the Royal Anthropological Institute, is shown here. References to the literature are given in the text of the paper. The author's surname (unless it occurs in the text), year of publication, and page number are enclosed in parentheses: "(Crooke 1926: 367)." An alphabetized bibliography at the end of the paper supplies complete information in the following forms:

Journal reference

```
Linton, R. 1943. Nativistic movements. Am. Anthrop.
45, 230-40. [When printed the volume number appears
in bold type. Thus in the type-written form the
volume number should be underlined with a wavy line
and "bold" written in the margin.]
```

191

Book reference

Crooke, W. 1926. <u>Religion and folklore of northern India</u>. London: Oxford Univ. Press.

MEDICINE

12:19   The *British Medical Journal,* the periodical of the British Medical Association, uses this style:

Journal reference

[4]Sheehan HL, Whitehead R. The neurohypophysis in post-partum hypopituitarism. <u>J. Pathol</u> 1963; 85:145-69. [The volume number is printed bold.]

Book reference

[5]Cox DR. <u>The analysis of binary data</u>. London: Methuen & Co Ltd, 1970:10-25.

PSYCHOLOGY

The British Psychological Society recommends the following:

Journal reference

Atkinson, J.W. (1957). Motivational determinants of note-taking behaviour. <u>Psychological Review</u>, <u>64</u>, 359-372.

Book reference

Gagné, R.M. (1977). <u>The Condition of Learning</u>, 3rd ed. New York: Holt, Rinehart & Winston.

CHEMISTRY

12:20   The Chemical Society uses the following style in its publications:

Journal reference

[10]W.T. Miller, J.H. Fried, and H. Goldwhite, <u>J. Amer.Chem.Soc.</u>, 1960,82,3091. [In printed form the volume number is in bold type. Note the absence of an article title.]

Book reference

[16]L.F. Fieser and M. Fieser, 'Reagents for
Organic Synthesis,' Wiley, New York, 1967, p.1256.

MATHEMATICS

12:21   The citation method used in the publications of the London
Mathematical Society involves the listing of references in
numerical order at the end of the paper. Thus, indication of a
source in the text is simple: "[4;p.54]". Full references are
given thus:

Journal reference

5.   R.B. Jensen, "The fine structure of the
constructible universe", <u>Ann. Math.</u>
<u>Logic</u>, 4(1972), 299-308.

Book reference

4.   W.K. Hayman, <u>Meromorphic functions</u>, (Oxford
University Press, London, New York, 1964).

PHYSICS

12:22   The citation system employed in the publications of the
Institute of Physics is characterized by succinctness, absence
of periodical article titles and lack of punctuation:

Journal reference

Cartwright DC 1978 <u>J.Appl.Phys</u>.49 3855-62 The volume
number appears in bold type in the printed form.
[Note that indication of this reference in the text
is merely "(Cartwright 1978)".]

Book reference

Holland R and EerNisse EP 1969 <u>Design and Resonant</u>
<u>Piezoelectic Devices</u> (Cambridge, Mass.: MIT) pp. 3-7

NUMERALS, SYMBOLS, AND ABBREVIATIONS

12:23   The demand in scientific papers for the use of numbers and
units of measurement expressed in numerical values makes it

suitable for purposes of clarity to use figures, symbols, and abbreviations to an extent not considered good form in nonscientific writing. Apart from a few rules here set down (paras. 12:24–27), the writer must settle on the scheme he will use, preferably when working on his first draft, and maintain the same usage throughout the paper.

12:24 Spell out a number at the beginning of a sentence, even if it is part of a connected group in which numerals are used after it. A better plan in such a case is to reconstruct the sentence so that it does not begin with a number.

12:25 Spell out expressions of measurement when they are not preceded by numbers.

12:26 To avoid confusion, you may spell out one set of figures in an expression that involves two or more series of figures:

```
In a test given six months later, ninety-seven
children made no errors; eighty-two made 1-2 errors;
sixty-four made 3-4 errors.
```

12:27 Do not use the symbol for *per cent* (%) when it is not preceded by a figure. And note that *percentage*, not *per cent* or %, is the correct expression to use when no figure is given:

```
The September scores showed an improvement of 70.1%
[or 70.1 per cent if the writer prefers the word to
the symbol]. Thus the percentage of achievers in the
second test indicated . . .
```

12:28 In mathematical texts the demands for the use of symbols and abbreviations are so complicated, and vary so much from one paper to another, that no suggestions can be given here. Reference should be made to The Royal Society. *General Notes on the Preparation of Scientific Papers*, to the same society's *Quantities, Units, and Symbols,* and to the British Standard concerned with the *Preparation of Mathematical Copy and Correction of Proofs* (BS 1219M: 1961). Editors of some of the mathematical periodicals have prepared manuals for authors which give useful suggestions.

13   Typing the Paper

13:1   The writer is responsible for the correct presentation of his paper in its entirety, that is, all the preliminary, illustrative, and reference matter as well as the main body of the text. Beyond the production of an accurate transcription of the copy, the typist should be held responsible only for mechanical details having to do with spacing, neatness, and the general appearance of the final copy.

13:2   Although this chapter is designed especially to guide the typist, it does not contain all that he or she needs to know in order to produce a paper in acceptable final form. Familiarity with the greater part of this *Manual* is necessary. Some rules for dividing words at ends of lines are given in chapter 3 (paras. 3:35–51). Two chapters, "Tables" and "Illustrations", require the typist's close attention, since the nature and complexity of illustrative materials demand that the writer of the paper be given virtually the same information for the preparation of his original copy as that needed by the typist who sets up the final copy. To avoid duplication, that information is not repeated in this chapter on typing.

TYPEWRITER

13:3   Either pica or elite type, or one of the types available on some of the newer typewriter models, is satisfactory for most

195

typing jobs, although some institutions specify pica type for theses and dissertations. A typist who expects to do any considerable amount of typing of theses, dissertations, or other formal papers, particularly those designed for submission to publishers, would do well to be prepared with a specially equipped typewriter, preferably with pica type. The special vertical spacing obtainable with the five-line ratchet is recommended for the typing of copy that is to be reproduced by one of the modern photo-copying processes (such as Xerox), and it may be used for any other copy, subject to the approval of the person for whom the copy is to be prepared. The same ratchet permits single and double spacing, and the accurate half-space turn of the roller is a great convenience in the typing of superscripts and subscripts. Keys with the grave accent mark (`), the acute accent mark (´), the circumflex (ˆ), the plus symbol (+), the plus-and-minus symbol (±), and the square brackets ([]) are almost indispensable. For the correct expression of the more common foreign accent marks, see chapter 4, para. 4:34. Some of the symbols carried on the standard keyboard are used less frequently in the typing of formal papers than in commercial work and can be replaced with the more necessary symbols.

13:4   Both type and rollers should be kept clean. Periodically, a thorough check of the typewriter should be made by a responsible serviceman to ensure smooth rollers, uniformity of letter impression, alignment of letters, and proper adjustment of tension.

RIBBON

13:5   Ribbons of superior quality are most satisfactory in the long run. Medium-inked black ribbons produce greater uniformity of impression than the light-inked or the heavy-inked. To secure superior uniformity of type colour, it is desirable to have on hand before the typing is begun enough ribbons of the same kind to complete the job, and to rotate them at regular intervals, of, say, every twenty-five pages. This is particularly desirable in typing copy for photocopying. Most electric machines use a one-time carbon ribbon which produces copy of extremely high quality.

PAPER

13:6   A good grade of bond paper should be used. Do not use one of the so-called erasable papers, unless it is specified by the institution to which the paper is to be presented. Some institutions have specific requirements for theses and dissertations. If there are no such requirements, paper of 20-pound weight and at least 50 per cent rag content should be used. Some institutions permit a lighter weight, or even machine copies, for the carbon copies.

CARBON PAPER

13:7   The carbon paper should be of good quality: black, hard finish (non-greasy), light- or medium-weight (light-weight is preferable if several copies are to be made). Such carbon paper makes a grey rather than a black impression, but the letters are sharper, and the copies smudge less and remain in good condition longer than those made with paper of a soft or medium finish.

13:8   The use of carbon paper on which the lines are numbered in a vertical column visible at the right of the typing paper is preferred by some typists to the guide sheet mentioned below (see para. 13:28).

CORRECTIONS AND ERASURES

13:9   No interlineations, crossing out of letters or words, strike-overs, or *extensive* erasures are permissible. A correction fluid, such as Correx correcting fluid, when properly applied, is satisfactory for making corrections.

13:10   Deletion or addition of more than one letter after the line has been completed should be made by retyping. By skilful use of the back-spacer, the letters of a word can be crowded so that the space normally occupied by a word of given length can be made to accommodate a word having one more letter. This must be done by erasing the entire word and reducing evenly the space between the letters, not by crowding just two letters. Extensive correction of a page once passed calls for great care

197

in retyping so that the material may be equalized and the last line on the page properly spaced out to the end. Erasures should be reduced to a minimum and made with such skill on both the original and the copies that they will not be noticeable. Wherever possible they should be made before the page is removed from the typewriter. Typists should form the habit of looking over each page before removing it from the machine. Once withdrawn, each copy of the set should be corrected separately by direct type rather than all together by restacking and insertion of carbons. Care should be taken to strike the keys heavily or lightly, as the case may require, so that the corrected portions may match in colour as nearly as possible the remainder of the typed material upon the page.

13:11 An erasing shield and two ink erasers—one with a broad edge for covering larger areas and one with a narrow edge for the smaller ones—are indispensable. To prevent smudging of the face copy, the fingers should rest on the erasing shield. To prevent smudging of the carbon copies, a piece of paper should be placed between each sheet of carbon and the page beneath.

13:12 Corrections on copy prepared for one of the modern photo-copying processes must not be made by erasing. A correction fluid, such as Correx correcting fluid, or a correction paper, such as Correx or Tipp-Ex correction papers, may be used. If errors on copy for photo-copying are not corrected by such methods, the corrected word or words should be retyped on a separate piece of paper and placed over the errors, attaching with a light coating of white casein glue (see para. 11:23). Great care must be taken to place the patch accurately and neatly and to leave no dark lines or specks which would show in the printed copy. Typing the corrections on white gummed paper is an alternative to typing on plain paper and pasting.

TYPING THE FRONT MATTER

TITLE PAGE

13:13 See paragraph 1:3 and example of title page (sample A, p.10).

TABLE OF CONTENTS

13:14   The writer of the paper is responsible for the content and style of the table of contents (see paras. 1:4–10). The samples shown in chapter 1 (pp. 10–15) illustrate four styles of tables of contents. Matters of spacing and alignment to be observed by the typist are:

The heading TABLE OF CONTENTS (or CONTENTS) is centred on the twelfth line from the top of the page.

If the paper is divided into PARTS, the part number and title is centred above the chapters they include (samples B and D).

Vertical spacing is as follows: *Triple* between TABLE OF CONTENTS (or CONTENTS) and first entry, and between PART and preceding entry. *Double* between PART and the following entry, between chapter headings, and between chapter headings and the first entry of a subheading. *Single* between individual subheadings (See samples B and C.)

A heading of such length that it would extend beyond the point of the last leader is divided and the runover is aligned vertically with the preceding line (see samples B and C). For the heading of a part, however, which is centred upon the page, the turnover is also centred (sample B). And for a subheading, the turnover is indented three spaces.

Chapter headings begin on the third space after the full stop following the chapter number, or of the last numeral of the chapter number if there is no full stop.

Chapter numbers when expressed in numerals are so aligned vertically that the longest number begins at the margin (samples B, C and D). If the numbers are spelled out, the longest *word* begins at the margin. Thus if there are full stops following the numbers (these are optional), the full stops will be aligned vertically:

```
     I.              One.
    II.     or       Two.
   III.              Three.
```

Leaders (rows of dots joining legends to chapter numbers) must always be aligned vertically, and there should be at least

199

three to four spaces between the last full stop and the first digit of the longest page number.

Page numbers are aligned vertically so that the last digit is next to the right-hand margin.

13:15   If a table of contents including both chapter headings and subheadings must be continued to a second page (or more), arrange the material so that if possible a major heading and all its subheadings appear on the same page. An exception may be made when a complete chapter unit is long, but in no case should a major heading be placed at the foot of a page with fewer than two lines of subheading (two lines, not necessarily two subheadings) beneath it. Begin a continuation on the sixth line from the top of the page and omit any heading (such as, TABLE OF CONTENTS—CONTINUED or CONTINUED).

13:16   If a table of contents occupies less than a page, the entire body of material should be approximately centred vertically upon the page. (See para. 11:25 for an interpretation of centring). The heading, however, should never be set higher than the twelfth line from the top of the page, and the space between the final line of typing and the bottom of the sheet should never be less than one inch.

LIST OF ILLUSTRATIONS

13:17   The writer of the paper is responsible for providing copy for the list of illustrations (which may be headed simply "Illustrations"). If in addition to figures, the list includes another designation such as "maps" or "charts" or "diagrams", and the list so designated is not too long to be accommodated on the same page with the list of figures, that list may either precede or follow the list of figures, depending upon its length. (See paras. 1:11–12 and sample G.) The heading should appear on the twelfth line from the top of the page, or lower if the list is short (see para. 11:25). Leaders (rows of dots) connect the individual legends with page numbers.

LIST OF TABLES

13:18   As reference to the sample lists in chapter 1 (pp. 14–15) will show, the list of tables is similar in style to the list of illustrations. (See para. 1:13 and sample H.) The heading, which may be "Tables", omitting the words "List of", is typed on the twelfth line from the top of the page, or further down if the list is short (see para. 11:25).

TYPING THE TEXT

MARGINS

13:19   Leave a margin of at least one inch on each of the four sides of the sheet. Some institutions require more than this, particularly on the left, since binding reduces the margin. On the first page of every major division of the paper (see para. 13:23), leave two inches at the top above the heading (i.e., begin typing on the twelfth line from the top).

INDENTION

13:20   Indent paragraphs six to eight spaces, unless other specific regulations are made. Follow the same scheme of paragraph indention consistently.

SPACING

13:21   The text should be typed either double space, one and one-half space, or a spacing provided on some of the newer typewriters that is somewhere between one and one-half and double space.

SPACING AFTER PUNCTUATION

13:22   Leave one space after commas and semicolons, and after colons except in scriptural references, and between hours and minutes, (Rom. 8:14–20, 4.30 p.m.), and except in such instances as in paragraphs 2:5, 3:42, 3:47, where more spaces may follow the colon. Leave two spaces after punctuation ending sentences. Do not space after periods in such abbreviations as i.e., e.g., a.m., p.m., A.D., B.C., U.S., N.Y., B.A., Ph.D.; but leave a space after periods following initials of personal names, as J. R. C. Stewart. Distinguish between a hyphen and a dash, which on a typewriter is made with two close-spaced hyphens. Leave no space before or after hyphens or dashes:

```
Midland is a fast-growing city.
```

```
The scheme proposed may--in fact, does--meet all the
stated requirements.
```

MAJOR HEADINGS

13:23   Begin every major division (i.e., contents, preface, list of tables, list of illustrations, introduction, each new chapter, bibliography, appendix) on a new page. Centre the heading in capital letters on the twelfth line from the top of the sheet. If the paper is divided into sections termed "chapters", the chapter number appears alone (e.g., "CHAPTER I") on the twelfth line, and the chapter title is centred on the third line beneath it. If the word *chapter* is not formally expressed and the sections are merely numbered, the number and title (e.g., "I. THE WORLD OF 1815") are centred on the twelfth line. If the title is longer than 48 spaces, set it in two (or more) double-spaced lines, in inverted-pyramid form. Use no punctuation at the ends of lines. Begin typing the text or the first entry of a list (contents, etc.), on the third line below the heading.

SUBHEADINGS

13:24   (For capitalization and style of subheadings see paras. 1:18–19.) A centred subheading of more than 48 spaces should be divided into two or more single-spaced lines, in inverted-pyramid form. A side heading of more than a half line should be divided more or less evenly into two (or more) single-spaced lines, the runover beginning at the margin. Paragraph headings should be underlined and should end with a full stop. All other subheadings should omit punctuation at the ends of lines.

13:25   All subheadings begin on the third line below text. If two (or more) subheadings appear together (i.e., without intervening text), a double space (blank line) should be left between them, and a double space left also between the subheading and the text following.

TYPING THE FOOTNOTES

SPACING, INDENTION, FOOTNOTE NUMERAL

13:26   Separate text and footnotes with an unbroken line twenty spaces in length, beginning at the left-hand margin on the first line beneath the text. The first line of footnote material is on the second line below this (the third line under the text). Indent the first line of each footnote the same number of spaces as the paragraph indention in the text. Type the footnotes single space, but use double space between individual notes.

13:27   Place the footnote numeral slightly above the line (never a full space above). There should be no punctuation after the numeral and no extra space between it and the first word of the note:

[1]Gabriel Marcel, The Mystery of Being, 1,42.

Since some typewriters lack the numeral one, the small "ell"–1–is used in its place, in footnotes and elsewhere. The capital "eye"–I–should be used only for the roman numeral one, never for the arabic 1.

ESTIMATING SPACE FOR TEXT AND FOOTNOTES

13:28   To place the footnotes correctly on the page and maintain the proper margin at the foot of the page, a *guide sheet* should be used. A special carbon paper may be used (see 13:8) or a sheet may be made of firm, light-weight wrapping paper. Cut it the same length as the typing paper and one-half inch wider. Measure off top and bottom margins to correspond with those used on the typed page, insert the paper into the typewriter, and, beginning with "1" on the line with that occupied by the first line of text on the typed page, number down the extreme right-hand edge of the guide sheet to the line opposite that of the last line of typed matter. It is helpful also to indicate in the top and bottom margins of the guide sheet the point opposite which the page number should appear (see paras. 13:38–41).

13:29   Before rolling the paper and guide sheet into the typewriter, place the guide sheet beneath the bottom sheet of typing paper; align the top and left-hand edges of paper, carbon paper, and guide sheet so that the numbered edge of the guide sheet extends beyond the typing paper; and roll the stacked paper into the typewriter. It may be necessary to adjust the top edges after the paper is placed in the machine.

13:30   When the first footnote number appears in the text, stop and count the number of lines in the corresponding footnote, add two to allow for the line of separation, and deduct this total from the total number of type lines as shown on the guide sheet. The difference between the two figures will give the number of the line at the end of which to stop typing text in order to allow proper space for the footnote. As each succeeding footnote number appears in the text, add the number of lines in the corresponding footnote, allowing one extra for the space between notes, and again determine the number of text lines to be typed.

13:31   All will go according to plan, and the bottom margin will be the proper depth unless a footnote number occurs in the last line of text after all available footnote space has been allotted. Make it a habit to look ahead so as to discover such a difficulty in advance, and avoid the necessity of retyping the page by omitting the last line, even though this will result in a bottom margin deeper than usual.

CONTINUATION OF A LONG FOOTNOTE

13:32   A similar difficulty arises when a footnote number shows the corresponding footnote to be longer than can be accommodated in the space remaining on the page. This calls for a division of the footnote.

13:33   Begin the note on the page where reference to it appears in the text and type as much as the page will allow, taking care to break the note within a sentence. Carry the remainder into the footnote area of the next page, where it precedes the footnotes for that page. To indicate the continuation of a footnote by such a statement as "Continued on the next page" is bad form.

ARRANGEMENT OF SHORT FOOTNOTES

13:34   To avoid the unattractive appearance and the waste of space which result from the placement of many short footnotes, each on a line by itself and separated from its fellows by extra space above and below, it is advisable to let such short notes follow each other on the same line. There must, however, be at least three spaces between notes, and *all the notes on one line must be complete*:

> [1]Kirk, <u>Keats</u>, p. 37.   [2]Ibid., p. 42.   [3]Ibid.

It is not permissible to carry over to the next line a part of the last note. Similarly, it is not permissible to utilize the blank space following a note of more than one line in length to insert a short note.

> <u>Wrong</u>:   [1]Duff, <u>Literary History of Rome</u>, p. 2, [2]Ibid. p.180.
>
> <u>Right</u>:   [1]Duff, <u>Literary History of Rome</u>, p. 2, [2]Ibid., p. 180.
>
> <u>Wrong</u>:   [1]Gabriel Marcel, <u>The Mystery of Being</u>, 2 vols. (Chicago: Henry Regnery Co., 1960). [2]Ibid., 1,6.
>
> <u>Right</u>:   [1]Gabriel Marcel, <u>The Mystery of Being</u>, 2 vols. (Chicago: Henry Regnery Co., 1960). [2]Ibid., 1,6.

ARRANGEMENT OF FOOTNOTES ON A SHORT PAGE

13:35   When the final material of a chapter is contained on part of a page, any footnotes applicable to the page should be arranged in the usual style after the space and separating line, immediately below the text.

ARRANGEMENT OF FOOTNOTES IN A QUOTATION

13:36 When a single-spaced, indented quotation includes one or more reference indexes from the source being quoted, the corresponding footnotes should be placed beneath the quotation, separated from the last line of the quotation by an eight-space rule (i.e., striking the key for underlining eight times). The reference indexes and the footnotes should follow exactly the form used in the original (see para. 6:11). References added by the writer of the paper should be numbered in sequence with the paper's notes and the footnotes placed at the bottom of the page.

TYPING THE REFERENCE MATTER

13:37 (For typing appendices, glossary, and list of abbreviations, see paras. 1:24–26.) In a bibliography, entries may be typed single space, double space, or one and one-half space. If single spacing is used, there should be a double space between entries. Each item should begin at the left margin and succeeding lines should be indented a definite number of spaces. (In the sample entries shown in chapter 8, the indention is six spaces, i.e., typing begins at the seventh space.) If desired, the authors' names may be typed in capitals throughout. Annotations should begin a new line and should be typed single space (see para. 7:33).

PAGINATION

13:38 Assign a number to every page of the paper except the blank sheet following the title page. On the title page (and the part-title pages, if there are any) the numbers are not shown, but the pages are counted in the pagination.

13:39 For the preliminaries, number with small roman numerals (ii, iii, iv, etc.) centred at the bottom of the page on the fifth line above the edge. The numbering begins with "ii"; the title page counts as page i, unless there is a frontispiece, which becomes page i, the title page ii. These numbers do not appear, that is, they should not be typed on the pages.

13:40   Number the remaining parts, including text, illustrations, appendix, and bibliography with arabic numerals, centred at the top of the page on the fifth line below the edge, except that on every page with a major heading (e.g., the first page of a chapter, of the bibliography, etc.), place the number at the foot of the page, centred on the fifth line above the edge. Begin the numbering of the main body of the paper with "1" and run consecutively to the end.

13:41   An alternate scheme of pagination is that of numbering all pages in the upper right-hand corner—excepting of course the title page and part-title pages.

SAMPLE TYPESCRIPT

13:42   The following two pages reproduce a typescript showing the opening pages of a chapter.[1] The text is double spaced; the block quotations and the footnotes are single spaced. The paragraph indention is eight spaces. The block quotations are indented four spaces in their entirety; if one quotation had begun with a paragraph, the paragraph indention would have been another four spaces.

[1]The sample pages are taken from a 1954 Ph.D. dissertation by St. Clair Drake, "Value Systems, Social Structure, and Race Relations in the British Isles" (University of Chicago), and are reproduced here with the kind permission of the author. Footnote style of the original has been altered to follow current practice.

CHAPTER II

THE DEVELOPMENT OF A RACE RELATIONS

ACTION-STRUCTURE

<u>Race Relations in the British
Isles: 1700 to the First
World War</u>

2 inch margin

12th line

15th line

17th line

20th line

21st line

22nd line

From the defeat of the Spanish Armada in 1588 until the abolition *24th l.*

of slavery throughout the British Empire in 1833, the economy of Britain

was tied, in some measure, to the fortunes of the African slave trade. In

the colonies of the West Indies and the southern United States, and later in

South Africa, black plantation labour produced wealth that flowed home to

Britain. In Britain itself, slave labour did not take root, although retired

planters and a rising commercial middle class sometimes used slaves as

servants. A small Negro population was living in London by 1700, and some

sources have estimated that by 1770 there were between 14,000 and 20,000

Negroes residing in greater London out of a total population of some

123,000.[1] They were mainly slaves and domestic servants living in white

45th l.

47th l. [1]This would be about the same percentage as Negroes constitute of
the present Chicago population. Little cites these estimates (Kenneth L.
Little, <u>Negroes in Britain: A Study of Racial Relations in English Society</u>
(London: Kegan Paul, Trench, Truebner & Co., 1947), p. 170), but notes that
C. M. MacInnes, in <u>England and Slavery</u> (London: J. W. Arrowsmith, 1934),
"doubts if the total slave population in England ever rose above 15,000 or
at most 20,000". One of the leading authorities on the social history of
the period, M. Dorothy George, puts the number of Negro slaves at "between
14,000 and 15,000". She states that "a large proportion of these must have
been in London, where they seem to have lived chiefly in the eastern and
riverside parishes." (See M. Dorothy George, <u>London Life in the XVIIIth</u>

homes, and of their relations with whites of their own class, one student

has written:

> . . . colour sensibility as such was very little in evidence. . . .
> No doubt Negroes in general were thought of more as slaves and servants
> than anything else, but there appears to have been no aversion to meeting
> or mixing with a person simply on the ground of his colour. [1]

During this same period there were about 10,000 Irish and 20,000 Jews in

London. Hostility toward them was great, and one student has said:

> All foreigners in London who had an outlandish look were likely to be
> roughly treated, or at least abused, by the mob. Jews were very
> unpopular. . . . Jew-baiting became a sport, like cock-throwing or bull-
> baiting, or pelting some poor wretch in the pillory. [2]

There were individuals among both the adherents of Conservative and

Liberal-humanitarian ideological systems who felt that, even though slavery

flourished in the colonies, it should not be permitted on British soil.

There were others who felt that the slave trade, if not slavery itself,

should be abolished. One zealous figure, Granville Sharp, through a series

of court cases, was able to have slavery on British soil declared illegal,

by judicial act, in 1772. But the Negro population referred to above con-

tinued to persist, and even to increase. Negro slaves from the West Indies

often attempted to jump ship and claim freedom because they were on British

soil. Of these individuals who were claiming sanctuary, one magistrate wrote:

> . . . they [slaves] no sooner arrive here than they put themselves on a
> footing with other servants, become intoxicated with liberty, grow
> refractory, and either by persuasion of others, or from their own
> inclinations, begin to expect wages according to their own opinion of
> their merits. [3]

Century [New York: Alfred A. Knopf, 1926], p. 131.)

[1] Little, Negroes in Britain, p. 203.

[2] George, London Life in the XVIIIth Century, p. 132.

[3] Little, Negroes in Britain, p. 176.

Appendix 1
Compiling an Index

Theses, dissertations and research papers do not usually require an index. Should the special nature of the work, or the requirements of the institution to which the work is being submitted, dictate that an index be compiled, the following will be found useful:

Anderson, M. D. Book Indexing. Cambridge
    Authors' and Printers' Guides. Cambridge:
    Cambridge University Press, 1971

Although this is a pamphlet it contains all the information that would be required to produce a soundly compiled index.

For fuller treatment consult:

Knight, G. Norman. Indexing, The Art of:
    a Guide to the Indexing of Books and
    Periodicals. London: George Allen & Unwin,
    1979.

This is a thorough and witty book produced by a founder member, first Secretary and subsequently President of the Society of Indexers. Among other things it reprints BS 1219C: 1958 *Notes on the Use of Symbols for Correcting Proofs.*

Appendix 2
Correcting Proofs

Corrections should be made as legibly as possible in ink (ballpoint is acceptable). Instructions to the printer which are not to be set in type should be encircled. The use of the more common correction marks is illustrated by the examples on pp.212 and 213, which have been taken, by permission, from *General Notes on the Preparation of Scientific Papers* (Rev.ed. 1974), published by the Royal Society, London.

[Proof]

Mark	
1. *s.c.*	**Results**
	Most of the experiments in the present
2, 3.	investigation were carried out with th
4.	cocaine/ and the results to be described
5, 6. *below/w.f.*	~~bleow~~ were obtained with this unless
7. #	special mention is made.
8. *ital*	<u>Magnitude of action potential.</u>
9, 10.	(1) <u>Conduction along the distal ~~non~~ non/</u>
11.	<u>narcotised segment</u> In view of the
12. *rom*	finding of (Woronzow) that the size
13. *trs*	the of electric response suffers decrement
14. *trs*	along the distal region most beyond the
15. =	depressed area, it is interesting, first
16. *see*	of all, to ~~find~~ whether the same
17, 18. *the/l.c.*	would occur under present (EXPERI-
19. *run on*	MENTAL) conditions.
20. *caps*	For this purpose dd leads were first
21. *less #*	employed. Records L of L propagated
22. *stet*	disturbances were taken ~~both~~ before and
23. ×	at varying intervals during narcosis and
24. *n.p.*	recovery. With ND leads diphasic re-
	cords ...
25.	Smith (1940) stated, The following
	general equation may be used

26, 27, 28.

$$a = K\alpha\beta \left[\frac{p+q}{(r+s)} \right]$$

To printer
l.c. sloping
Greek kappa

Meaning of marks

1. Change to small capitals
2. Invert letter.
3. Close up.
4. Substitute comma. (Similarly for semicolon.)
5. Replace by word in margin.
6. Wrong fount. Replace by letter of correct fount.
7. Insert space.
8. Change to italics.
9. Delete (take out).
10. Insert hyphen.
11. Insert full stop. (Similarly for colon.)
12. Change to roman type.
13. 14. Transpose. When several words are badly mixed up they may be numbered, the mark 'trs' being written in the margin.

[The same corrected]

Most of the experiments in the present investigation were carried out with cocaine, and the results to be described below were obtained with this unless special mention is made.

Magnitude of action potential.

(1) *Conduction along the distal non-narcotised segment.* In view of the finding of Woronzow that the size of the electric response suffers most decrement along the distal region beyond the depressed area, it is interesting, first of all, to see whether the same would occur under the present experimental conditions. For this purpose DD leads were first employed. Records of propagated disturbances were taken both before and at varying intervals during narcosis and recovery.

With ND leads diphasic records...

Smith (1940) stated, 'The following general equation may be used

$$a = \kappa a_0 \left[\frac{p+q}{(r+s)^2} \right]$$

Meaning of marks (continued)

15. Straighten lines.
16. Replace by word in margin.
17. Insert word or letters in margin.
18. Change to lower case.
19. No fresh paragraph here.
20. Change to capital letters.
21. Reduce space.
22. Leave as printed.
23. Replace by similar but undamaged character.
24. Begin a new paragraph.
25. Insert single quotation mark.
26. Symbols over which this sign is placed to be 'inferiors' (subscripts).
27. Symbols under which this sign is placed to be inserted as 'superiors' (superscripts, indices).
28. Note to printer to explain an unusual character or expression.

213

Appendix 3
Useful British Standards

Although practice in this *Manual* does not always conform to the recommendations of the British Standards Institution it may be found useful to consult the following:

BS 1629: 1976		Bibliographical References.
BS 3700: 1964		Preparation of Indexes to Books, Periodicals and Other Publications.
BS 4148		Abbreviation of Titles of Periodicals.
	Part 1: 1970	Principles.
	Part 2: 1975	Word-Abbreviation List.
BS 4821: 1972		The Presentation of Theses.
BS 5261		Copy Presentation and Proof Correction.
	Part 1: 1975	Preparation of Typescript Copy for Printing.
	Part 2: 1976	Typographic Requirements, Marks for Copy Preparation and Proof Correction, Proofing Procedures.
BS 5605: 1978		Citing Publications by Bibliographical References.

Index

Index

Index

Quantities. *See* Measurements
Quasi, compounds with, 3:33
Question. *See also* Question mark within
    another sentence, 3:58
    polite request, 3:59
Question mark, 3:58–60. *See also*
    Question
  with ellipsis points, 5:16, 5:20
  at end of sentence, 3:58
  to indicate uncertainty, 3:60
  with quotation marks, 3:107, 5:15
  within sentence, 3:58
  spacing with, 13:22
Quotation marks
  colon with, 3:107, 5:15
  comma with, 3:107, 3:108, 5:15
  with correspondence, 5:11
  double and single, 5:9, 5:10, 5:14
  with ellipsis points, 5:16
  exclamation mark with, 3:107, 5:15
  in footnotes, 5:8
  with headings and subheadings, 5:13
  period with 3:107–8, 5:15
  punctuation with, 3:107, 3:108, 5:15,
    5:26–30
  question mark with, 3:107, 5:15
  semicolon with, 3:107, 5:15
  single, 3:108, 5:9, 5:10, 5:14
  for titles of works, 4:16–28, 5:10,
    6:31, 7:31, 8:20, 8:22, 8:32,
    8:45
  with words and concepts, 3:108, 5:10
Quotations. *See also* Block quotations;
    Quotation marks
  capitalization in, 5:1, 5:24–25
  ellipsis in, 5:16–32, 5:34, 5:36–37
  in footnotes, 5:8
  footnotes to, 6:11, 13:36
  foreign-language, 4:31–32, 5:32
  headings and subheadings within,
    5:13
  incomplete, 5:31, 5:35, 5:37
  indention of, 5:2, 5:33–34, 5:36
  internal punctuation in, 5:9
  interpolations in, 3:99, 5:39–42
  italics (underlining) in, 5:42
  of letters, 5:11
  of outlines, 5:12, 5:23
  of poetry, 5:3–6
  prose, 5:2
  within quotations, 5:14
  run into text, 5:2, 5: 5–6
  from secondary source, 8:27
  spacing of, 5:2–3

spelling in, 3:1 (see also *Sic*)
  terminal punctuation of, 5:26–30

Radio programmes, 3:48, 4:25, 6:117
Radio stations, 6:117
Reduction, photographic, 11:16, 11:29
Reference lists. *See* Bibliographies
Reference matter, 1:21–27. *See also*
    Appendices; Bibliographies;
    Glossaries
  placement of, 1:2
  typing of, 1:25, 13:37
References. *See* Bibliographies; Cross-
    references to specific pages;
    Footnotes; Reference matter
Regiments, 2:47
Religious names and titles, 2:6, 2:7, 7:19
Reports
  government, 9:15, 9:23, 9:24 (*see also*
    Official publications)
  published, 8:28–29, 8:42
  unpublished, 8:32
Reprint editions, 6:45, 6:62, 6:66, 8:19
Residence. *See* Address
Restrictive clauses, definition of,
    3:71–72
Reverend, 2:7
Ribbon, typewriter, 13:5
Roman numerals
  in classical references, 6:87, 6:113
  in footnotes, 6:73
  for front matter, 6:87
  in outline form, 2:57
  for parts of book, 6:87
  with personal names, 2:44, 7:22
  in references to pages so numbered,
    2:34, 2:35, 6:87
  for volume numbers, 6:87
Rulers, names of, 2:43, 6:134, 9:20
Rules
  for author's name in bibliographies,
    7:24, 12:9
  in tables, 10:16, 10:36–41
  between text and footnotes, 13:26,
    13:36
Runover lines, indention of, 13:14

Sacred writings. *See* Bible; Scriptures
Saint, with names, 2:8, 2:9, 7:15
Samples
  of list of illustrations, p. 14
  of list of tables, p. 15

Index